FROM PIGLETS TO PREP SCHOOL

Other Books by Wendell A. Duffield

Volcanoes of Northern Arizona:
Sleeping Giants of the Grand Canyon Region

Chasing Lava:
A Geologist's Adventures at the Hawaiian Volcano Observatory

When Pele Stirs:
A Volcanic Tale of Hawaii, Hemp, and High-Jinks

Poems, Song Lyrics, Essays, and Short Stories by Nina Hatchitt Duffield:
An anthology edited and annotated by Wendell and Anne Duffield

FROM PIGLETS TO PREP SCHOOL

✦

Crossing A Chasm

Wendell A. Duffield

iUniverse, Inc.

New York Lincoln Shanghai

FROM PIGLETS TO PREP SCHOOL
Crossing A Chasm

iUniverse books may be ordered through booksellers or by contacting:

iUniverse
2021 Pine Lake Road, Suite 100
Lincoln, NE 68512
www.iuniverse.com
1-800-Authors (1-800-288-4677)

The places and people described in this book are real. The events are accurately described within the limitations that come with the hazy memory of a sexagenarian and his sparse decades-old notes. Given human nature, individuals mentioned in the story may remember events somewhat differently than I do. If anyone feels misrepresented, I apologize for whatever the unintended error may be. In spite of my best efforts to avoid mistakes, some of the relative timing of events may be wrong. I confess to practicing a smidgen of "poetic license" where minor flights of fancy add interest but no harm to the story. If any of my French friends bristle at how I characterize the fairly widespread disdainful French attitude toward our American culture, I'm sure we can talk our way through such a triviality.

ISBN-13: 978-0-595-37569-1 (pbk)
ISBN-13: 978-0-595-81963-8 (ebk)
ISBN-10: 0-595-37569-3 (pbk)
ISBN-10: 0-595-81963-X (ebk)

Printed in the United States of America

I dedicate this book to Gary Gardner. He was a cherished friend and frequent companion during the early formative years of our growing up. We shared many adventures before a series of post-cards from H. Hamilton Bissell uprooted me from a bucolic life in Browns Valley, Minnesota, and transplanted me into the rather snobbish garden of New England preppies at Phillips Exeter Academy, in Exeter, New Hampshire. Later in life, while I was chasing volcanoes for my career, Gary was a truck driver working out of Browns Valley. I stop to reminisce with him whenever I get back to the old hometown.

Contents

List of Illustrations ix

Foreword. xiii

CHAPTER 1   Pigs On The Loose!! 1

CHAPTER 2   Wobegon And Other Lakes. 11

CHAPTER 3   The Scent Of Money Drifts In 17

CHAPTER 4   The Idea Pans Out 24

CHAPTER 5   Wintertime Blues 33

CHAPTER 6   It Took A Village. 44

CHAPTER 7   The Bissell Epistle 54

CHAPTER 8   Harley's On Hold 67

CHAPTER 9   Food For Thought. 73

About The Author 75

List of Illustrations

Gertie, Wanda, and Rocky look-alikes at about three months old. Photo by Lewis P. Watson, in the Lewis P. Watson Collection at the Olivia Raney Local History Library, Wake County Public Library System, Raleigh, NC 27610. Used with Library permission. 6

For Gary and me, the lumberjack shake seals a deal. Photo of Jack Hereford (right) and Ben Mathis by Richard Hereford. 9

The outflow channel (River Warren) for glacial Lake Agassiz. This channel merges with the flat bed of glacial Lake Agassiz a couple of miles north of this image. The smaller channel in the upper left part of the image was also once a drainage for Lake Agassiz. Today the town of Browns Valley (BV) lies at a north-south continental drainage divide. Water flows north from Lake Traverse (LT) and south from Big Stone Lake (BSL). The small hill at the south edge of BV is the gravel bar where the Browns Valley Man was buried. 12

The buildings of Uncle Clare's farm are set into the wall of the valley of River Warren. The long straight road across the foreground marks the hill where my sister Thalia and I nearly perished in a harsh Minnesota blizzard during the winter of 1955/1956. Oblique aerial photo from Duffield family archives. 18

This mother has more babies than milk spigots. Photo by Akos Jung. Used with his permission. 20

Gary and I seal a deal with a farmer handshake. Hands of Jack Hereford (cow) and Ben Mathis (milker), photographed by the author. 23

Gary and I took the runts while these better-fed look-alike siblings stayed with mom. Public domain photo. 25

Hand-written receipt for the sale of our first batch of hogs. The scrawl under the heading "Remarks" is Arnold Kaus's version of bu, which is his shorthand for butcher hogs. From Duffield family archives. *31*

Color it maroon, add a layer of dust and some dents that come with being seventeen years old, and you have an image of the car that I learned to drive in...a 1936 Lincoln Zephyr sedan powered by a V-12 engine capable of moving the rig at ninety miles per hour. Image compliments of the Ford Motor Company. *33*

Hand-written receipt for the sale of our second batch of hogs. Two of the four weighed so little (220 pounds total) that they carried the label of ltbu (light butcher hogs). Mr. Kaus did the long division for us, to show how to split the money fifty-fifty. From Duffield family archives. *48*

I'm starting to ponder a plan of animal-raising diversification to make money for buying a Harley Davidson. Jack Hereford photographed by the author. *53*

Pam Mutchler look-alike at lamb feeding time. Photo provided by Linda Singley, Bearlin Acres Farm, Shippensburg, PA. Used with her permission. *68*

ACKNOWLEDGMENTS

I thank my friend Rosemary Hume, a Flagstaff, Arizona, teacher of the city's Unified School District, for prodding me into writing about something other than volcanoes. Her 2003/2004 crop of sixth-grade students critiqued a pre-publication version of this book as an exercise to help them master the English language on a path of training for the exams now required for graduation from high school. Each of these young students provided remarkably cogent and insightful suggestions, which led to additions and significant improvements to an early version of the manuscript. Jack Hereford (son of Sue Beard and Richard Hereford) and Ben Mathis (son of David and Christine) agreed to pose as models for Wendell Duffield and Gary Gardner, respectively. Sue and Richard provided editorial comments on an early version of the manuscript and some of the photos of the young boys that appear in this book. My dear mother had the foresight to save for decades such seemingly unimportant documents as receipts for the sale of pigs raised by Gary and me. Without these pieces of faded paper, I would be guessing today at the market weight of our pigs and the price per pound that we were paid for the animals some fifty years ago. I thank Linda Singley for her diligent search of dusty closets to find an old photo of a lamb being bottle-fed. Thanks to Professor Mark Lehner (University of Chicago/Harvard University) for recently reminding me that long ago he "burglarized" my family home. You can read about this in chapter 1. Today, as a world-class archaeologist, he continues the practice of snooping in the homes of others by supervising digs into the dwellings of the ancient Egyptians who helped build the pyramids at Giza. Mark Manone and Jana Ruhlman helped with the digital illustration of the landscape around my hometown. My shirttail cousin Jim Lammers saved me from the potential fate of boiling in a pot of legal oil. As usual, my wife Anne was sounding board, editor, and overall supportive spouse throughout the writing process. My friend Louella Holter added a professionally polished job of final editing.

Foreword

You may wonder why a retired elderly geologist would write a non-geologic book that he hopes will appeal to young readers as well as adults. This geologist never had children of his own, biological or adopted. But he's always enjoyed the company of youngsters (even after many experiences as a baby sitter!), and of course he once was one himself, during a blissfully simple earlier part of his life. My motivation for writing about those days now, in the autumn of my years, arises from two very different sources.

Number 1: Recently, I've been entertained and inspired by reading Gary Paulsen's fascinating book ("How Angel Peterson Got His Name") about his experiences growing up in a small Minnesota town…a town not far from where I grew up.

Number 2: I've been encouraged to write for pre-teen and early teen readers by a talented and enthusiastic veteran teacher (Rosemary Hume) whose classroom I've visited many times during the past decade, to talk with her students about my thirty-year career as a volcanologist. In fact, Rosemary's the person who introduced me to Paulsen's books.

So, there you have it; some chitchat with a friend and a little reading-for-pleasure have driven me to a computer keyboard to reminisce about my youthful years.

Time and again during recent months, I've found myself identifying with the tales spun by Paulsen, often to the point of eye-watering laughter. He and I grew up in very similar Minnesota environments, at almost exactly the same time. Life in rural Minnesota differs little through time and space, to be sure. Paulsen is a wildly successful author, and I figure that if I can write about my childhood shenanigans half as engagingly as he writes about his growing-up adventures, I may have a second career in store. You, the reader, will be the judge of that possibility.

Besides, retirement should not mean…well…assuming a retired posture while idly consuming space and other valuable resources of our finite world. Retirees have much to offer society if they will get off their collective duffs and keep their creative juices flowing. There should be much more to life after sixty than golf, cards, shuffleboard, and gambling.

What can I add about Rosemary? She's a bundle of energy and is always on the lookout for written materials to use in her classroom. She's one of those "hidden" treasures in a public school system that often under-appreciates, or fails to properly recognize, talented employees who put in an extra non-required effort. For some reason, Rosemary believes that I can produce books that will help activate the gray matter of her students and encourage them to be increasingly inquisitive...to make them *want* to learn, rather than *have* to learn in order to advance toward graduation. I find it more than a wee bit incredible that she has already found some of my popular *geological* writings of use to this end in her classroom. Her confidence that my writing abilities may extend to topics other than rocks, minerals, and volcanoes is remarkable and daunting.

I welcome the challenge, though, simply because I'm still a child at heart. The calendar says I'm a sexagenarian, a word that carries a somewhat oxymoronic connotation I won't explore further here. Yes, I have many friends who are my contemporaries in calendar time; and yes, these are mostly serious people imbued with adult thoughts and utterings. But my psyche seems to be stuck somewhere in the teenage years. Given a choice, I often prefer sharing ideas with a civilized teenager to talking with a sophisticated adult.

Maybe I'll eventually "grow up" enough to voluntarily wear something other than blue jeans and tee shirts and to choose to discuss the weighty matters of state, politics, ethics, and religion. Meanwhile, though, I prefer to try to stay young, in part by reliving my early years through writing short stories about being young. If you got this far, you're on your way to reading the first one. Writing about childhood times takes me back vicariously to those formative years. Those were fun times...times of playfulness, learning, innocence, a little craziness, and some sadness. Writing about them is an effective way for me to ride a time machine back to the 1950s. I hope you'll join me on this journey.

1

Pigs On The Loose!!

"Mom! Mom!!" my younger sister Jackie yelled as she crashed through the screened-porch door. It slammed shut loudly behind her. She burst through the open kitchen door, and slid to a stop at the middle of the room where our mother was stooped over a small oak table, working a lump of bread dough toward a tasty addition to an evening meal that would feature meat and potatoes. Jackie's pair of nearly waist-length tightly braided pigtails flapped like twin leather whips as she ran, head bobbing up and down. Her hairstyle couldn't have been more appropriate to the tale she was about to tell. "Mom! Those pigs that Wendy and Gary are raising got out of their pen again. This time they're in Reverend Lehner's vegetable garden!"

Judging from the tone of her voice and the expression on her face, it was impossible to tell if Jackie was acting out the role of a snippy little sister tattling on her brother, or was genuinely concerned for the Reverend's garden. But if she was in fact worried about the garden, wouldn't she have chased the pigs away before running home? Whatever Jackie's motive may have been, Mother took the kind-and-understanding approach to the shouted news. Her brood of one son and five daughters between the ages of seven and seventeen generated more than enough inter-sibling competitions in the form of verbal and sometimes physical fights often ending in tears, without her taking a side that might lead to yet another childish argument.

She looked up slowly from her work, hands not breaking their steady rhythm of fold-squeeze-push-roll on the dough. "Thank you, Jackie. It's nice that someone is keeping track of those animals." As a way to help project calm where a storm might be brewing, she continued working the ball of dough against the flour-sprinkled tabletop before placing the squishy white orb at the center of the table, where she covered it with a clean cotton hand towel decorated with the image of a smiling Rosie the Riveter of World War II fame. Rosie was flexing her biceps and her words "We can do it!" were captured in a cartoon thought-cloud.

As Jackie fidgeted, Mother wiped her hands on her apron. Unlike Rosie's neat-and-clean pink cheeks beaming up from the rounded top of the covered lump of dough, the apron was decorated with a chaotic profusion of colorful food stains accumulated from the inevitable spills that occurred while cooking for eight people each day. She walked slowly toward a far corner of the kitchen, where a closed door hid the foot of a stairwell that led to the old Victorian house's second level.

"Hurry, mom!" was written all over Jackie's face.

My best friend Gary and I were in my bedroom, sitting on a small army cot, thumbing through collections of baseball cards. With carefully planned trading among friends and between ourselves during the past couple of years, we had accumulated identical sets of cards...one hundred and thirteen each. We kept them in alphabetical order by the last names of the players, so we could easily find a particular card and quickly compare our sets. We weren't sure how many cards made a complete set, but we knew we had a ways to go before getting there.

"Dang! We still don't have the Musial card," I complained. Stan Musial was one of the most popular players with all young baseball-card collectors. "We've gotta keep buyin' gum so we can get a Musial."

"Yeah, sure," Gary replied. "But where'll we get enough money to buy all that gum?"

We each opened a new packet of the stuff and started chewing it up into a malleable wad. "Rats! Another Al Kaline. Wha'd you get?"

"Ditto," said Gary. "He's a pretty good hitter. But a right fielder...what a wimpy position to play."

The gum we talked about was all one brand. Each packet of pale pinkish Dubble Bubble bubblegum came with a card. It seemed that the company selling Dubble Bubble purposefully packaged very few Musial cards with their jaw-strengthening product as a way to get kids to buy more and more gum whether they wanted something to chew and get creative with, or not. We knew we'd have to buy a lot more Dubble Bubble if we ever hoped to score a Musial. We needed ways to earn enough pennies to get every different card.

"Let's go search the ditches along the highway again for pop bottles. We haven't done that for a week, and people are always throwing their empties out the car window. Pop sellers still pay a penny an empty...one more shot at a Musial." Our money-making scheme was loudly interrupted.

"Wendy!" Mother had opened the stairwell door and was shouting up the narrow walkway. "Wendy!"

I exchanged "aw, crumb" eye contact with Gary. "What, m o o o o m?" I answered in the plaintive unenthusiastic tone of voice that kids use when they don't want parents butting in on their fun.

"You and Gary come down here right now. Those pigs of yours are in Reverend Lehner's garden. You'd better get over there fast and hope they haven't destroyed too many of his vegetables. I swear those animals do nothing but chew and swallow twenty-four hours a day. It's easy to see where the phrase 'eats like a pig' comes from. Come on now, get a move on!"

We exchanged another "oh, darn" glance, put our card collections back in their safe-keeping boxes, shoved them under the bed, and hit the floor running…popping pink bubbles on the move. We'd been through this pigs-on-the-loose drill before, though not when our animals were in a neighbor's garden. They usually preferred to search for edible goodies in the grassy ditches that bordered town streets.

Raising the pigs was a summer project to help us earn lots of extra pocket money. We figured that once the pigs were sold at the end of the summer, the Stan Musial cards should be within easy financial reach, even if they were rare as hen's teeth. Once we each had a Musial, we planned to move on to scoring a Duke Snider card, which seemed to be as scarce as the Dubble Bubble Musial. Of course, Snider *might* show up first.

"We're on our way, mom," I shouted as we ran through the kitchen and out through the screened porch. Once again the familiar sound of that door slamming shut pierced the air. Isn't it remarkable how much physical abuse a feeble-looking screen door can tolerate without collapsing into a pile of pieces! "Don't worry. We'll catch 'em real quick."

The Lehner place was a block away. We streaked in that direction, after a short detour to our detached garage where Gary and I kept pieces of rope designed for pig-catching occasions. From a distance, we could see the critters of our summer project slowly browsing through the garden, undisturbed and unaware that their morning brunch was about to be cut short.

All was quiet as we ran past the Lehner house. Apparently no one was home. Being Saturday, Reverend Lehner may have been across town at the Presbyterian Church, writing his sermon and making other preparations for tomorrow's service. In a town whose population was barely a thousand, yet was served by churches of six denominations, competition for parishioners was keen. Captivating sermons were an important recruiting tool, although the promise of faith healing and emotional group "dancing" seemed to be the most-successful recruiting tools at the Holy Roller church…a dilapidated cement block structure set into a hillside. The building looked more like a potato cellar than a place of serious Christian worship.

Who could know where Mrs. Lehner and her growing batch of young Lehner kids might be...or what they might be up to. In good-natured observation of the obvious, neighborhood scuttlebutt labeled the family the Chaos Clan. But then, most of the scuttlebutters weren't exactly paragons of neat-and-anal organization themselves.

Closer now, Gary and I saw that two round, hard-flesh porcine snouts indented with twin nostrils were easily uprooting a variety of delicacies. It was late summer. The veggies were ripe and tasty. Soft and rhythmic sounds of oink oink oink, punctuated by the occasional crisp snap of a fresh vegetable bit through, reflected a high degree of diner satisfaction. As was colorfully plain to see, the pigs especially preferred bright orange carrots, deep purple beets and stark white potatoes...a messy rainbow of colors like those on Mother's apron. The occasional chaw on a pea vine apparently served as fresh green salad. Thorny raspberry bushes were being ignored. Luckily for the Lehner sweet corn, ripe and juicy ears were high enough up their stalks that the pigs weren't yet aware of their favorite yellow food dangling tantalizingly nearby. Corkscrew-shaped pig tails were twitching in delight as jaws worked nonstop.

"Gary." I paused long enough to create a professional pink pop. "You take Gertie. I'll get Wanda."

Gary and I liked to name things...our tricycles, bicycles, sling shots, cap guns, Red Ryder BB-guns, as well as living things like our pet dogs and of course the pigs. We'd named Gertie after Gravel Gertie, an unattractive bug-eyed female character in the Dick Tracy comic strip that we both loved. Wanda's namesake was a secret that only the two of us shared. One of our classmates at school wouldn't be happy if she knew how we associated her with Wanda. I suppose we were just acting like normal boys at our almost-teenager level of maturity. Girls were still in the yuck category of people classification. We didn't realize it at the time, but our view of girls would soon change from yucky to yummy as certain adolescent stirrings set in.

Like every other garden in town, the Lehner vegetable patch wasn't fenced. As Gary and I walked onto the edge of the garden, Gertie and Wanda lifted their heads, jaws and tails still moving, in recognition of their keepers. They immediately went back to eating. They weren't about to run. Even though they were an in-town version of a farm kid's 4-H project...meat on the hoof on the way to market...they were practically obedience-trained family pets. We looped our ropes around their necks without a chase and were leading them back to their pen when that young boy sense of play and competition kicked in.

"Hey, Gary. Bet I can beat ya to the pen. Whatta ya say?"

Pop...pop. He stalled long enough to get the exploded part of his wad back in his mouth. "No way," he shouted, as we swatted the butts of Gertie and Wanda to get them moving at top speed across the Lehner lawn, the two of us barely keeping up at the end of our ropes.

Pigs were squealing in delight and we were yelling to distract each other, when I stumbled over a Lehner-boy toy, hidden in tall grass that needed mowing. I fell, but barely slowed in my race with Gary. At her two-hundred-pound late summer weight, Wanda dragged my less than hundred-pound body across the lawn with little effort. The steady rhythm of her galloping (do pigs gallop?) stride didn't miss a beat.

I could, and maybe should have let go of the rope and easily caught Wanda later, but what young kid wouldn't want to enjoy the extreme sport of being dragged across a lawn by a noisily gleeful pig! So instead, I kept a tight grip around a fist-sized knot at my end of the rope. I rolled dizzying spirals to the left and to the right behind a weaving streaking squealing Wanda as she accelerated to an ever-increasing speed. She sounded as thrilled as I felt. Wildly twisting pendulum-like swings back and forth across the grass gave me the idea that this kind of pig pull should become a new sport, added to the greased-pig chase that was a favorite activity for kids at the Traverse County Fair each fall.

About then and luckily for me I suppose, my lean...well, really just plain skinny...body proved to be enough of an anchor that a winded Wanda stopped at the edge of the gravel driveway separating the soft grass of the lawn from the fenced pig pen. She and I paused to catch our breath. I was gasping so hard that I almost swallowed my Dubble Bubble. Even motionless, winded Wanda continued to squeal in delight about the new sport. It must have been pig talk for "what a kick!" Meanwhile, I tried to bring double-vision back into single focus. Spinning at the end of the rope had addled my inner ear so much that I was too dizzy to stand up. I was a lightheaded happy-go-lucky product of the porcine version of the tilt-a-whirl ride at the Fair.

"Boy, mom's not gonna be happy about this" I mumbled when I finally got vertical on wobbly legs and looked down at a once white tee-shirt. Skidding through the grass had torn loose one of the two metal hooks that held up the bib of my farmer overalls to expose the shirt. Even the blue overalls were stained visibly green. But as someone who didn't have to help with the laundry chores (why should I, with a mother and five sisters to handle the load?), I simply grinned, coiled up enough rope to put Wanda on a short lead, scratched favorite pleasure-receiving places behind her ears, and got her walking across the gravel-covered ground to the pig-pen gate where Gary and Gertie were waiting.

"Ha! I beat you by a country mile" taunted a laughing, bragging Gary.

"Yeah, yeah, you won. But I had lots more fun!" I countered as we put Gertie and Wanda back into their half-a-town-block enclosure. Rocky, the third pig of our batch, had stayed in the pen, waiting by the gate for his friends to return. A satisfied "oink, oink" was hello to his pals. As a neutered male, a barrow in technical farmer talk, Rocky always was the lazy stay-at-home type while his "sisters" went gallivanting about our neighborhood at every opportunity. He was the porcine version of a eunuch, but he wasn't much of a guardian for his female pen partners.

Laid-back weakling though he seemed to be, we'd named him for a permanent fist-sized lump on his left side. Gary and I made up the story that he'd been punched hard there by a porcine Rocky Marciano. We kept that Rocky M's card, too, even though he was in boxing instead of baseball. He was a tough guy and one of our heroes; our four-legged Rocky was a reminder of that.

Gertie, Wanda, and Rocky look-alikes at about three months old.

As the already well fed Rocky watched, Gertie and Wanda shoved their snouts into a wet slurry of ground oats that sloshed from end to end in the feeding trough. Some of the white liquid was oozing from one end of the trough, so Gary and I stuffed our wads of gum into the wet crack. Several strips of pink against a beige pine background attested to other leaks that had been patched this way. Dubble Bubble was the duct tape of gums.

Gary nodded agreement when I said the obvious "we've gotta try to patch this fence again." We walked the pen's perimeter until we found where Wanda and Gertie had wriggled under the woven-wire barrier. To close that escape hatch, we piled the heaviest rocks we could carry onto the bottom strand of wire. From earlier experience, we knew the pigs would eventually find another place where they could escape to freedom. But only about two more months of this catch-and-pen game separated us from driving Gertie, Wanda, and Rocky to market. Then we'd have plenty of moola for Dubble Bubble and other treats.

"We better go back to the garden to see if we can fix the mess Wanda and Gertie made" I said, knowing full well it wouldn't take much of a detective to recognize that something was wrong no matter how hard Gary and I tried to heal the wounded ground. With a short detour to the garage, we exchanged lead ropes for rakes.

Back at the vegetable patch, we managed to rake away the most visible evidence of the pig-snout plowing. But in spite of our best efforts, a glaringly obvious lack of the above-ground leafy green parts announced sections of missing carrots, beets, and potatoes along carefully laid out rows of otherwise closely spaced plants. What could we do but mumble about maybe being in big trouble when Reverend Lehner noticed what the pigs had done?

Feelings of blue and worry about what the Reverend's reaction to this mess might be evaporated when I remembered a conversation overheard when he came to visit our house one night the previous week. I broke a smile, caught Gary's attention with a loud "hey," and waved him over.

"Ya know, Gary" I said, rolling that conversation around in my head, "I don't think we'll be hearin' from Reverend Lehner about this." I looked around to be sure no one had crept up within hearing range. "Here's why."

We kept raking as I shared my secret, in the low voice of a kid thinking he's a successful sneak. "The Reverend came to our house last week to apologize cuz his youngest son, Marky, broke into the place while we were away visiting relatives a few days earlier. Heck, no one I know ever locks their house in this town, so Marky just walked in…he didn't break in, cuz he didn't have to."

Gary cocked his head and studied my facial expression, trying to anticipate whatever it was I might say that would ease his uneasy feelings, too.

"Anyway, mom, dad, and Reverend Lehner searched our house together, upstairs and down. Afterwards, I heard my folks say that nothing of value seemed to be missing. They didn't know I was listening in and soakin' up their words, cuz I was sittin' next to the radio, pretending to pay attention to an adventure of the Green Hornet."

Gary's head shifted into a slow up-and-down nod as he began to see where my tale was going.

"Reverend Lehner was gushin' apologies right up to and out the front door. I could tell he was feelin' real guilty, even if Marky hadn't taken anything. So.... I don't think he'll make a stink about a few lost carrots and beets. Besides, isn't he supposed to practice what he preaches about 'turning the other cheek' and stuff? I say we're home free!"

We grinned at each other the way that only silly scheming young boys can do when they feel extra clever about pulling a fast one. "Let's sign off on this caper with a handshake."

We moved a few steps into the partial screening shelter of the back wall of the Lehner garage, to keep our handshake a secret from potentially prying eyes. We replaced grins with serious business expressions. I made a fist with my right hand, fingers grasping the vertically extended left-hand thumb. Then I gently curled the tips of my left-hand fingers. Gary did the same with his hands and turned to face me. With our curled fingertips interlocked, we moved our joined hands back-and-forth in the motion of a pair of loggers using a bucksaw. The lumberjack shake! What could be more appropriate in the home state of Paul Bunyan?

More pig-related adventures would round out that summer, before we had to go back to school. There'd be more secret handshakes for sealing deals and hatching schemes during the rest of our warm-weather fun. With one last knowing grin shared, Gary headed home for his noon-time meal, and I rounded the corner of the garage toward my place.

On the walk back, I gathered a bouquet of about a dozen dandelion flowers to give to Mother as a way to help soften what might be a less-than-pleased reaction to my grass-stained clothes. I'd presented a dandelion-bouquet gift before, and would do it again. Gazillions of dandelions grew everywhere around town, in spite of Herculean summertime efforts by proud homeowners to remove them from their lawns, if not from the very face of the earth. Still trying to rationalize what the pigs had done to his garden, I figured that harvesting the bouquet was a favor to Reverend Lehner, though the length of his grass suggested little concern for lawn care.

For Gary and me, the lumberjack shake seals a deal.

I entered the screened porch slowly, being careful to ease the door closed to keep it from slapping shut. I walked into the kitchen, bouquet-bearing hand outstretched. Mother smiled and purred a "thank you, Wendy" as she accepted my offering. I answered "yup and yup" to her questions about catching the pigs and trying to fix the garden.

She'd finished the pre-baking ministrations to bread dough and had moved on to peeling potatoes. She said nothing about my filthy clothes. Instead, smiling, she began to arrange the weed-flower gift in a small water-filled Mason canning jar, as artfully as a professional florist might do with roses in an elegant vase at a wedding. As she worked, sticky white sap seeped from the open end of the tubular stem of each dandelion and spread across her fingers. Finished, she wiped that juice on her apron, adding one more substance to the colorful mix already there. Hands clean, she positioned the jar at the center of a windowsill that was bathed in sunshine and was visible from all parts of the room. She stepped back and admired her creation, adding a "looks fine, don't you agree, son?" In another setting, she might have just put the Hope Diamond on display in a magnificent circular glass case at the Smithsonian Mineral Museum.

I basked in pride about the bouquet and was wallowing in relief that my grass-stained clothes weren't mentioned. As skillfully as Roy Rogers regularly managed to avoid being shot on the silver screen during Saturday matinee movies, I had dodged yet another potentially wounding scolding well deserved for my messy ways.

Though *I* never kept score, my sisters liked to remind me about an enviably successful track record of dodging these bullets. "You practice dandelion bribery with those bouquets for mother," they would whine. I, of course, liked to think that my intentions were honorable, even if a bouquet was occasionally (often?) used to distract attention from having created extra work for Mother, in the form of stained clothes and other "accidents."

Whatever mind games may have been behind the custom, those bouquets became an important link in the relationship that developed between Mother and me as I grew up. Although most people consider dandelions to be noxious weeds, when picked and delivered lovingly by her only son, Mother always said that "a bouquet of these common yellow blossoms is the kindest and prettiest gift a mother could want. Why, a dandelion even *feels* good when you twirl it against the skin under your chin."

Much later in life, once I learned the meaning of the following *M* word, I came to understand that the simple act of my giving and Mother's cheerful receiving of the bouquets was a *m*etaphor for parent/child love and bonding. Mother and I still talk and laugh about those bouquets, a half-century after the Lehner-garden caper.

2

Wobegon And Other Lakes

A little information about the town where Gary and I grew up might ratchet the enjoyment index higher (I hope!) for readers of this pig story. I think Garrison Keillor would agree. Just about anyone who listens to National Public Radio is familiar with Keillor's Prairie Home Companion show. A key to much of the wild success of this show is easy-to-like, down-home entertainment that stems from listener familiarity with the people and places of Lake Wobegon, Keillor's "hometown."

A couple of decades before Keillor introduced radio listeners to the peculiarities of life in Lake Wobegon, a small imaginary village he's created near Freeport in west-central Minnesota, I was approaching my early teens, growing up in a dirt-street real version of his mythical place. The name of my town was, and still is, Browns Valley. This Minnesota town is "way out west"... about a hundred miles west of Lake Wobegon and a literal stone's throw from South Dakota.

In contrast to Keillor's lake town, Browns Valley boasts two lakes...Traverse to the north, and Big Stone to the south; parts of the town almost extend into the lakes and in fact do during spring-thaw flooding. These watery neighbors are shaped like gently curved fingers (or maybe like giant hot dogs, if you're a fantasizing hungry teenager), disfigured by an arthritic kink here and there. Each lake is many miles long but only a mile or so wide. Together they form a gigantic west-pointing bowlegged *V* on the landscape, an open *V* whose feet don't quite touch, where they converge toward Browns Valley. An imaginary line that traces the long axis of each lake marks the boundary between my home state and the wild-and-wooly southern version of Dakota. If you open your national road-map atlas to the Minnesota (or South Dakota) page you'll easily locate Browns Valley.

Speaking of water, a contemplative person familiar with Lake Wobegon might ask: "Are two lakes better than one?" After all, I've read and have been personally reminded during conversations (mostly with Parisian friends) about the widely held French view that we Americans are born with the notion "bigger (or more) is

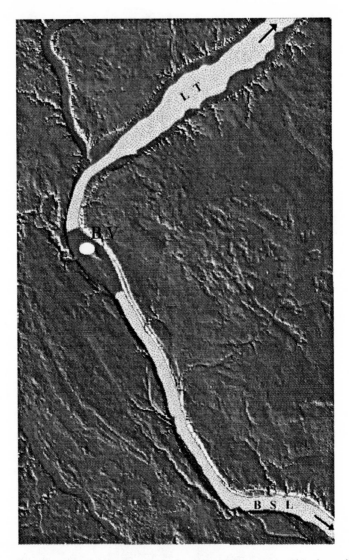

The outflow channel (River Warren) for glacial Lake Agassiz. This channel merges with the flat bed of that former lake a couple of miles north of this image. The smaller channel in the upper left was also once a drainage for Lake Agassiz. Today the town of Browns Valley (BV) lies at a north-south continental divide. Water flows north from Lake Traverse (LT) and south from Big Stone Lake (BSL). The small hill at the south edge of BV is the gravel bar where the Browns Valley Man was buried.

better" irretrievably embedded in our brains. Those freedom-loving Frenchmen, perhaps feeling uncomfortable by being constrained to live within the boundaries of an entire country only about the size of our state called California, may be partly correct about us. But even if size, shape, depth, water quality, and other factors were compared, the outcome of a two-lake-versus-one-lake contest could be debatable...and probably not important to the truly significant issues of life, anyway.

But sizes and numbers aside, what's extra neat about the lakes of BV (that's what all we locals have always called our town) is that even though they're rather shallow (in spite of being very long) and tend to turn green and slimy during late summer as algal blooms are increasingly nourished by fertilizer washed in from nearby farm fields, those lakes are steeped-in-history remnants of a huge river (Warren) that flowed from a gigantic gla-cial lake (Agassiz) about ten thousand years ago. Traverse and Big Stone are mere puddles, the residue of a raging ice-age river that was much larger than Brazil's Amazon. BV is located barely downstream from the point of origin for glacial River Warren.

Agassiz and Warren were waters to be reckoned with. Agassiz once cov-ered what later became part of northwestern Minnesota (submersing the future site of Gary Paulsen's hometown), a swath across eastern North Dakota, a little bit of northeastern South Dakota, and a whole lot of adja-cent Canada...an area that increased as North America's most recent gla-cier retreated northward with warming climate.

As a feature flowing across and beyond land that would later be named Min-nesota, Warren was a humongous river carrying a lot more water than today's Mississippi (or Amazon) does. It's not surprising then that big old Warren eroded itself a remarkable and sometimes meandering valley that extends southeastward from the BV area, across central Minnesota, and then southward from Minneap-olis to the Gulf of Mexico. Today, this valley is used by the Minnesota and Mis-sissippi Rivers...latter-day carpetbaggers whose waters don't come close to filling Warren's broad deep valley.

About nine thousand years ago, someone chose a River Warren gravel bar as the burial site for a man and his prized possessions. In 1933, the bones and arti-facts were accidentally discovered during excavation of a gravel pit at the edge of BV. This "Browns Valley Man" (Google him up on the Internet!) is one of North

America's oldest known humans. Like I say, old River Warren and its remnants of today are very special in many a way.

As a kid growing up in BV, I'd never heard the words *geology, glaciology,* and *archaeology*. It never occurred to me and my buddies to even wonder why the lakes were right there next to town in our cozy valley. But all of us kids surely appreciated those bodies of water. They provided instant expansive ice rinks for winter sports and were the prime source of cooling recreation during hot-and-humid Minnesota summers.

The dry valley at BV today is about two hundred feet deep, incised into the nearly billiard-table-flat surface characteristic of most of the Great Plains. Relative to those Plains, the walls of BV's valley are precipitous. I imagine that folks living among real mountains will laugh at the following half of this compound sentence, but flatlanders have been known to visit from miles away, just to ski and sled on BV's hilly surroundings.

Here's another landscape feature that makes BV special...something a first-time visitor probably would never guess without help. BV sits atop a continental drainage divide! When a raindrop falls at exactly the right position in town, half of it (in theory, at least) flows northward into Lake Traverse, which feeds the Red River of the north on its journey to Hudson Bay, while the other half flows southward into Big Stone Lake, which feeds the Minnesota River on its journey to join the Mississippi at Minneapolis.

Compared to the lofty razorback continental divide that snakes across high mountains in Montana, Wyoming, and Colorado, BV's continental divide is dreadfully subtle...and crests out at less than a thousand feet above sea level. I'm reasonably sure that Gary and I sometimes temporarily diverted Minnesota River water to the Red River, and vice versa, with our playful channeling of spring snowmelt runoff by dragging the heels of our snow boots across soft muddy ground, or by creating shallow drainage trenches with sandbox shovels. But wherever that subtle and sometimes mobile line of continental divide ran through my hometown during any given day or year, it was and still is within the city limits...as surely as the Red and Minnesota Rivers exist.

When the retreating glacier still covered a lot of southern Canada, water couldn't flow northward. But once that huge ice sheet melted back to its present-day position in the Arctic, the spot where BV would later grow became what is surely one of the world's subtlest continental divides.

With such interesting geological, archaeological, and geographical histories to boast, you may wonder why so few outsiders have ever heard of BV. Fact is, of course, the town is just another tiny rural farming community in a huge region dotted with similar settlements. Honestly, most of Garrison Keillor's descriptions of Lake Wobegon could just as well be applied to BV, the peccadilloes of the town's Scandinavians, Lutherans, local gossip and all. Being familiar with both, I can easily imagine that Millie's Cafe in BV provided Keillor with a model for creating Wobegon's Chatterbox Cafe.

When I was growing up there, local chatter claimed that BV was populated by more than a thousand people, and that number may have been accurate. During the half century since, though, the number has shrunk to around five hundred, as young folks have moved to "big cities" to find life-supporting jobs. My point is that BV has always been a small-town farming community, a place of reasonably comfortable living with neither the cultural advantages nor the grandiose and luxurious frills of a New York City, San Francisco, Minneapolis, or even Fargo just a hundred miles to the north…the nearest community that might be entitled to apply the word *city* to itself.

No one in BV was wealthy by American standards during my childhood years. But no one was living in abject poverty, either. Everyone had entirely adequate food, clothing, and shelter. And believe you me, soundly built and adequately insulated shelter was absolutely necessary on blustery minus forty degree (that one-and-only crossover point for the Fahrenheit and Celsius temperature scales) winter days. But there was so little money in town that could be directed to things other than the three necessities of life, that even a young naive kid like me was aware of potential poverty lurking around the next corner, or more likely, around the next marginal grain harvest. The town's economic health closely tracked the financial ups and downs of surrounding family farms.

Don't misunderstand me. I wasn't a whiner. My billfold wasn't empty in this frill-free society. I had a paper route that brought in a couple of bucks each week. In addition, my dad paid me thirty-five cents an hour to empty wastebaskets and generally clean his place of business (a Sinclair gasoline station) enough to keep it looking spiffy. Dad and Mother also rewarded me with dimes for *A*s and nickels for *B*s on the periodic report card during the school year. Looking back on those times, I suppose I was lucky that my parents didn't ask me to pay *them* for any *D*s and *F*s, *C*s being neutral ground.

But, it took precious little time to empty a few wastebaskets daily and to sweep a small floor; at thirty-five cents an hour…well, you do the math. Report cards were too infrequent and the number of graded subjects (five) too few to put much money in my pockets, even if I scored straight *A*s (once again, you do the math). Being a carrier salesman for the Minneapolis Star and Tribune was almost a losing proposition, because several of my customers created a seemingly infinite number of lame excuses for not having the cash to pay me when I made my monthly collection rounds. It's hard for a young kid to wrestle money from an unwilling adult. I could write an entire book about this unfair situation. But like a stoic businessman, I swallowed the loss and carried on...stiff upper lip and all that malarkey.

With my combined sources of income, I could maybe afford one movie with popcorn and soda per week. On a flush summer day, I could nibble at a five-cent ChoCho, a small cup of chocolate-flavored imitation ice cream, while my more fortunate friends made loud slurpy and sucking sounds announcing that the intake end of their straws were at the now-empty bottom of their tall malted milk containers. On other days, hanging out with friends at Agar's Cafe could be downright embarrassing. While buddies were ordering cherry or lime cokes, sometimes with a yummy chocolate sundae on the side, I was softly whispering my order for a pine float. Mr. Agar understood teenage peer pressure and tried to minimize an awkward situation by serving me a glass of iced water with a floating pine toothpick *after* my friends were so wrapped up in their tasty liquid delights that they didn't notice what I was consuming.

What self-respecting and even mildly proud kid could enjoy that scene? I wasn't a greedy little urchin, but I did pine for some financial security and independence, beyond my available means.

Maybe if I quit goofing off at Sunday School and stopped sleeping through monotonously droning Methodist sermons, some higher religious power would smile my way? Maybe I was simply overdue for a secular stroke of luck?

Maybe I was doomed to a childhood with darn few perks.

3

The Scent Of Money Drifts In

Surprise! Payoff came from an idea that *I* hatched, without apparent help from above or a gift from lady luck. The chance to hugely increase my pocket money wafted in on the fumes of pig manure one sunny weekend day during the spring of 1953. Pig poop and possible green backs. Squirming, squealing piglets and potential cash. What unlikely but welcome combinations.

On that propitious day, Gary and I were hanging out at my Uncle Clare's farm, watching a bunch of sows nurse their recently born litters. Uncle Clare's place was at the north edge of town, within easy walking distance. We often visited to see the wonders of farm-animal life in action, events that biology schoolbooks try valiantly, though often with limited success, to explain and illustrate with words and pictures.

Most of us have heard it said that "a picture is worth a thousand words." And there surely are situations where this aphorism applies. But, if you want to quickly and graphically learn about important events in an animal's life cycle, I recommend that you spend time on a farm, especially during breeding and birthing seasons. Seeing a dozen or so piglets emerge from a mother to take their first independent breaths and then immediately stumble on shaky short legs toward a milk-giving teat is far more instructive than words or pictures in any textbook. Gary and I had seen many piglets born during the past few years (lambs, calves, and colts, too), most recently just days earlier. Today was a follow-up visit to see how the little porkers were doing.

Uncle Clare's farm buildings were set into the wall of River Warren's valley. Gary and I climbed up this gentle hill to a red rectangular wood-frame shed that served as the pig-birthing place. When we entered, Uncle Clare was on the opposite side of the room, doing a routine check of the mothers and their litters. Hearing the shed's door open and close, he turned toward us. An instant smile replaced serious concentration on his face.

17

The buildings of Uncle Clare's farm are set into the wall of the valley of River Warren. The long straight road across the foreground marks the hill where my sister Thalia and I nearly perished in a harsh Minnesota blizzard during the winter of 1955/1956.

"Hi, Uncle Clare," I began. "How're you today?"

"Wel l l l l l. Hello, Wendy and Gary." Uncle Clare had a neat way of combining a friendly laugh with his talk, as though he had two sets of vocal cords that he used simultaneously. "I'm doin' fine. How're you two?"

I turned my head away and grimaced. Zounds, I hated that nickname. A boy with a girl's name…a name right out of Peter Pan, for crying out loud! But it wouldn't be polite for me to complain to Uncle Clare. My mother and dad (Uncle Clare's brother) had formally named me Wendell, which had been shortened to Wendy before I could even talk or walk, I'd been told. And Wendell wasn't even a family name, just a parental pick from the *W* section of an alphabetical listing of possibilities. Why couldn't Dad and Mother have selected Daniel, or Thomas, or Michael, or any number of other "regular" names like my friends had? But how does a young kid tell his parents that he hates his name, the full or shortened version? For the time being I was Wendy. The only cool thing was that the initials of my full name (Wendell Arthur Duffield) described the soft and elastic pink stuff Gary and I chewed on almost constantly.

I gently bit my tongue in silent frustration and turned back toward Uncle Clare. "We just dropped by to see how the new piglets are doin'. Is that okay?"

"Sure," he replied. "Snoop away. Just remember the things I've told you about being careful with the sows." Uncle Clare went back to his work while Gary and I drifted toward different pens.

The shed was full of wiry-haired, rusty-red Duroc sows mothering recently born litters. A somber hospital quiet filled the space, save for the occasional low-pitched oink of a satisfied-sounding mother, and the high-pitched staccato squeals of piglets in search of food. The air was bittersweet with the mixed odor of oat straw partly saturated with pig urine and poop. Doors and windows were kept closed to keep out the early spring chill. Each sow had her own space, about six-by-twelve feet, defined by four-foot-tall wood-slat partitions. The mothers were on their sides, exposing teat-lined underbellies to hungry piglets. Each mom weighed in at about three-hundred-fifty pounds, and each baby weighed only a pound or two.

I tucked my toes between the bottom two slats of a pen, so I could step up and drape my arms and shoulders over the top board and watch littermates vie for a place at the source of milk as mother lay calmly nursing. She seemed pleased with what was happening to her. I was tempted to jump in and pet the cute little critters, but Uncle Clare had long before made it clear that Gary and I should stay out of the pens. Some local farmers had scars as proof that the mothers can be fiercely protective of their new babies. The jaws of an adult pig can easily crush walnuts and apricot pits, to say nothing of the bones of a human hand.

Uncle Clare kept moving about the shed, while humming the tune and words that I recognized as "Son of the Soil," one of many songs that his mother, my Grandma Duffield, had written. Uncle Clare loved to sing his mother's songs. Today's remembered tune seemed entirely appropriate as he methodically checked to see that moms and kids had plenty of comfortably clean straw bedding, and that a mom wasn't about to roll onto one of her litter. The outcome of that kind of mishap was obvious.

One of the little porkers I was watching wasn't getting her lunch. I began counting the babies…fifteen of the little suckers…and then mom's teats. There was a mismatch…fifteen piglets in need of sustenance and only ten teats.

That's when my mind's light bulb clicked on, dimly at first, illuminating a nascent idea that might lead to a moneymaking venture. I started to toss that idea around silently, making a mental list of pluses and minuses.

"Uncle Clare." He was on the opposite side of the shed, still humming, with his back to me. He didn't respond until I raised my voice enough to be heard over the background chorus of porcine grunts and squeals. "Uncle Clare. This mom has too many babies for the number of her feeding places." He turned and walked toward me.

At my age, it wasn't proper to use the word teat in adult company, even though I knew exactly what teats were on a new mother…milk spigots. I'd heard that many kids born and raised in big cities believe that milk comes from a carton. We farm-country kids knew that cartons were way down the assembly line of milk production. As I've already said, a farm is a great schoolhouse for lots of plant and animal information. The life-giving function of a milk-filled teat is a topic impossible to ignore during birthing season.

This mother has more babies than milk spigots!

Uncle Clare stepped up beside me and looked down at the head of the sow. Her right ear was tattooed with 36. A successful farmer needed a foolproof way to identify individual breeding animals in order to establish an accurate record of their life history, most especially their productiveness during times of birthing and rearing. Uncle Clare was one of the most methodical and successful farmers in the county. With his right index finger bobbing up and down in sync with barely audible counting, he ran his own census for number 36 and her litter.

"You're right, Wendy."

My shoulders drooped in a silent uuuugh! There was that hated name again.

"Having fewer teats than babies isn't unusual with pigs. And old number 36 has quite a record of doing this. She's one of my most productive sows."

We watched together for a few minutes as the littermates pushed and jockeyed for the ten food-dispensing positions. Most of the piglets were able to complete several sucking swallows before being pushed aside by an aggressive sibling. But one piglet, noticeably smaller than the rest, wasn't making contact with mom.

"Usually the babies work it out among themselves so they all get enough milk to thrive til they're able to handle solid food," Uncle Clare added.

Amid the concert of high-pitched squeals, the scrawny one was never able to push her way to mom. In the rough and tumble world of survival of the fittest, scrawny spent as much time on her back as on her feet. Both Uncle Clare and I saw what was happening.

"Sometimes there's a weak little runt like this one," he continued, "who can't get enough milk. Weak runts usually starve. It's just a fact of life, or death in this case, when raising pigs. I have a few of these every year."

Uncle Clare went back to his rounds as I thought about that for a while, all the time watching the weakling continue to fail to push her way into and past the writhing throng of her successfully nursing siblings. I was pretty sure that there was nothing wrong with the runt that food wouldn't cure. She just needed a little nursing. My mental light bulb was glowing brighter.

With an attention-getting "psssst," I waved a come-over-here signal to Gary, who was peering into another pen. We went outside for private talk. "Hey, Gary. Did ya hear what Uncle Clare was telling me in there?"

Before answering he breathed in deeply, covered his right nostril with his right thumb, closed his mouth, and blew out hard enough to clear the drippy beginnings of a cold from his left nostril. Success. He switched thumbs and sides, breathed in, and blew again. Though we were "townies" in local lingo, we thought of ourselves as farmers, and this was classic farmer nose blowing while in the field. We practiced the farmer blow a lot. It made us feel way cool. Sissies used handkerchiefs.

"Yeah, so?" mumbled Gary as he wiped the back of his right hand across his nostrils and then along the seam of his right pant leg. That farmer blow could be messy at times.

It was my turn to act out the role of farmer. Wearing bib overalls certainly helped. I unhitched the metal clasp of the over-the-shoulder strap on my right, letting that flap of the bib flop down. I shoved my left hand into a pocket as deeply as I could reach, where I kept a few nails and a coiled piece of baling wire. Following a few seconds in serious selection, I pulled a long stalk from a tall grassy weed with my right hand, and used the plant's stem to clean between my front teeth...natural dental floss. With an appropriate backdrop, my pose could have been used to advertise Funks G Hybrid corn or some other agricultural product.

"Think about this," I began. "If a runt pig is gonna die anyway, just because it can't push its way to a teat, what if we saved it by hand-feeding milk made from powder? Uncle Clare doesn't have time to hand feed the weaklings, but you and I do. We could end up with the pig version of a cash cow, if we could take a runt, raise it to market weight, and sell it."

Gary hitched his thumbs around the straps of his bib overalls. A smile formed slowly across his face, like maybe his idea light bulb had clicked on, too.

"Why the heck didn't we have this idea before?" I continued. "Think of the possibilities. With money from sellin' a market pig, we wouldn't have to order any more pine floats. And we could see all the movies and slurp all the malts we'd want! Who knows? There might even be some money left over." We were both getting excited by mental images of extra pocket money.

Following a few more minutes of supposing and planning, punctuated by farmer-style kicks at dried cow patties during lulls in conversation, we agreed to pursue the pig project. But there was one more thing to do before our plan was official. Staring intently at Gary, I interlaced the fingers of my hands and pointed my thumbs down, palms facing him. He reached out to grab my thumbs and gently tugged at each one, alternately, making the motions of milking a cow. Thumbs for teats, we both made the *schush-schush-schush* rapid-fire sound of squirts of milk being added to a partly filled pail.

The pact was now sealed with our secret farmer handshake. We grinned like the silly kids we were, while somehow believing we were adult enough to launch into the serious business of raising pigs.

"Let's do it!" we shouted in unison.

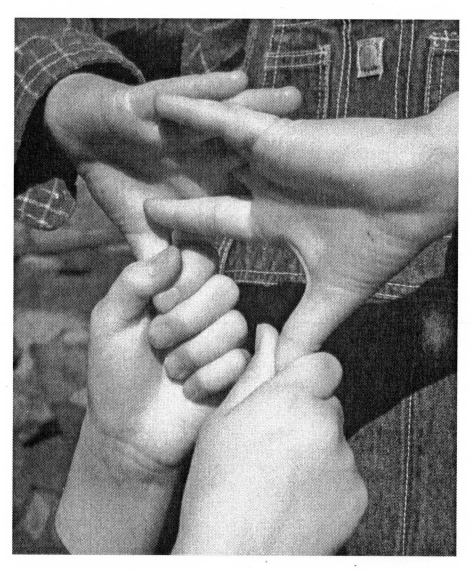

Gary and I seal a deal with a farmer handshake.

4

The Idea Pans Out

Uncle Clare would have to agree to our plan if it was to advance. And since he was my uncle, it was my job to convince him to give us that runt. Heading toward the shed's door, I mentally rehearsed an approach that I thought might work on an uncle known for his great sense of humor. Gary stayed outside during the negotiations…the silent business partner.

When I entered the shed, Uncle Clare was looking into the pen with the weakling. I shuffled quietly up beside him, formed a facial expression of grave concern, and did my best vocal imitation of Mr. Beaulieu, BV's one and only mortician and funeral director. His quiet-and-deferential manner was widely known, and expected, around town. No one wanted an overly enthusiastic funeral director at the farewell ceremony for a loved one. Though of tall and imposing stature, this man could retreat into nothingness, ghost like, when standing next to a filled coffin.

"Uncle Clare, do you really think that poor baby pig is gonna die?" I asked softly. I paused long enough for the idea of death to sink deeply into his mind.

"I'll bet all she needs is some food. I mean she's…she's probably not really sick or anything. She maybe just needs a chance that…that her selfish brothers and sisters aren't giving her."

I was feeling rather proud of my Beaulieu-like, sympathy-saturated whisper. I'd even managed to include a hitch or two in my voice that projected a sense of barely stifled sobs. I was simultaneously serious and play-acting, reliving a mix of stage roles I'd filled at church pageants and secular public-school events. Uncle Clare looked at me with increased interest and apparent concern.

"Look, Wendy. I think you're right. The little one probably could be saved, given enough milk. But I don't have time to nurse individual weaklings. I have too many other chores to do to keep the farm going. I'm sorry when weak runts like this one die, but that's just the way it is."

From his tone of voice, I got the impression that Uncle Clare was feeling at least a little bit concerned, if not guilty, about the probable fate of the runt unless some human intervention took place. It was time to propose *the idea*. It was definitely *not* the time to be feeling sorry for myself about hearing my sissy nickname again.

"Well, if you're pretty sure the runt is gonna die, what if Gary and I took her home and hand fed her until she was stronger? If we got her to put on a little weight, and maybe even got her to where she could eat solid food, then she could rejoin her family."

Uncle Clare looked thoughtful for a few seconds. "I'll tell you what, Wendy. If your folks will agree to let you try to hand raise this runt at your place, you and Gary can take her and keep her. I've got nothing to lose, and you two might have several worthwhile things to gain. This'd give you a chance to raise an animal from a baby, to learn the responsibility that goes with doing that, and to maybe even make some spending money if you can get her up to market weight by this fall. Go home and ask your mom and dad."

I grabbed Uncle Clare by the arm, jumped up and down, and yelled "Wow!" Suddenly my funeral-director demeanor was as dead as a funeral-director client.

"Hush," Uncle Clare cautioned. "You'll spook the sows."

"I'm sorry. And thanks, Uncle Clare. I'm going home right now to see what dad and mom say."

When I burst out the shed door in full grin, Gary knew that we had the green light. Together, we ran down the hill into town, half-hooked overall bibs flapping in the breeze.

Gary and I took the runts while these better-fed look-alike siblings stayed with mom.

That was Saturday. By Sunday afternoon we had three scrawny-looking piglets in our care. You met them as mature animals in Chapter 1...Gertie, Wanda, and Rocky. Uncle Clare had discovered two more weaklings, from a different litter, that probably also would die if left to fend for themselves.

Dad designated a corner in our garage as an okay place for a piglet pen. For their house, we set up the taller part of a cut-off cardboard shipping box for a refrigerator...instantaneous roof and four walls. A foot-square hole cut into the base of one side served as doorway when piglets wanted to explore outside their house. A couple of one-by-ten boards tacked together at right angles, with free ends set snugly against walls near a back corner of the garage, created an "outside" enclosure to keep the piglets from wandering away. Spring nights were still chilly, so we carved a small hole through the top of the cardboard house, through which we fed an electrical extension cord to a heat lamp that hung safely above straw bedding. *Piglet Palace* was cozy and comfortable. We wrote that name on the side of our cardboard creation in tall, bright-red, block letters.

We fed our brood milk made from powder formulated specifically for piglets. Voracious appetites were evident. Weight gain was obvious within a week, as the protruding outlines of thin-and-curved ribs disappeared into fleshy bodies.

We garnered neighborhood fame as kids from blocks around streamed in to see what we were up to. Friends wanted to pet the piglets (they were cute and friendly little things) and help feed them. Volunteer labor was in surplus.

Within a month, the porkers had outgrown their inside house and pen. They were also ready for solid food. Gary and I had to get creative, if we were going to be able to continue our project and show a profit by fall. I started to mumble as we watched *Piglet Palace* being pushed atilt.

"Whada we gonna do?" The cardboard house in the garage was easy to build, but now we had bigger animals to worry about. As luck would have it, the space part of a solution to our growing needs was right across the street.

Two contiguous empty city lots became the outdoor pigpen. This land laid smack dab between the Duffield and Gardner houses and was even fenced with the four-foot-tall woven wire that any farmer would use for a pigpen. It was the perfect location from our point of view, and it was free. We (and our parents) didn't know whose land it was, but no irate owner appeared even after our pigs' presence was obvious.

We built a V-shaped feeding trough from equal-length scraps of two-by-ten planks by nailing a rectangular board across each end of the V, and moved the pigs to their new spacious home. They gleefully wallowed in their newfound freedom to roam far beyond the space that *Piglet Palace* had provided. In spite of all the new space, though, the expectable waste droppings of digested food accumulated a bit faster than they disintegrated. On the positive side of the ledger, the classic oink oinks of rapidly growing and self-satisfied porkers entertained the neighborhood with porcine arias.

Patti Paulsen, however, was not entertained. She lived in a rented room of Garmen Peickert's house, northwest across the street from the pigpen. Patti was of courting age, and was regularly entertaining an eager suitor whom she feared might be put off by the sight, sound, and most especially the smell of nearby pigs as a prelude to a date. Gary and I often heard her complaints as she stood at the house door, waiting for her beau to arrive.

"Jeeze, wheeze. What a crumby deal! Here I am trying to land a husband, and I have to do it through the stench of pig poop. Mom never told me romance would be this tough in a two-horse town like BV. I wish I only had two horses to put up with, instead of three stinkin' pigs."

Fortunately (for Gary and me), the Peickert house was sufficiently upwind that this lovely romantically smitten young lady never lodged a formal complaint with local authorities. We did have a couple of close calls though when the pigs somehow rooted their way under the fence and roamed neighborhood ditches in search of food before we discovered their illicit freedom.

You've already read about the pigs-in-the-vegetable-garden caper of later that summer. Reverend Lehner never did scold us. Ironically, as an adult his son Marky made a professional career of snooping in other people's homes by acquiring a PhD at Yale and then supervising archaeological digs into the dwellings of the Egyptians who had helped construct pyramids at Giza.

As another unfortunate result of an episode of free-roaming pigs, Patti's suitor, Merv Zabel, managed to flatten a pile of fresh poop with a brand new size-nine penny loafer, when he chanced to step out of his car exactly where that smelly stuff had been recently deposited. But this mishap didn't dissuade Merv from going on with his date, which was just one more in an increasingly hot romance that soon led to marriage. A puzzled passerby reported seeing Merv rubbing his right shoe frantically back and forth across tall grass in the ditch that evening. Gary and I came to understand why Merv had done this dance, once we heard about his impromptu last-minute shoeshine through BV's grapevine gossip.

In sharp contrast to Patti were Claude and Fern Roark, a retired farm couple who lived adjacent to and directly downwind from the pen. They enjoyed the pungent reminder of their earlier years. This couple was truly salt of the earth…perhaps better described as people of the earth. They preferred the natural odors of land and animals to the artificial essence of eau de toilette used by the upwind courting couple.

When pig appetites outgrew a steady diet of milk, Gary and I found a source of solid nourishment at Palmer Hansen's feedmill. The mill was where farmers brought truckloads of grain to be ground into a fine white powder used as animal food. The routine went like this: A truck offloaded its grain (oats, wheat, barley, or corn) into a hopper that funneled into a machine with steel grinding teeth and plates. The empty vehicle was then repositioned beneath a nearby loading chute, where the ground grain was fed into the truck a few minutes later. No matter how carefully this routine was played out, some of the feed spilled onto the concrete-slab floor beneath the truck. The amount spilled was too small for a farmer to bother with. Mr. Hansen, however, was delighted to have Gary and me clean up the spillage on a regular basis; otherwise he would have to do it…and he had no pigs to feed.

We had our source of free solid food, and Mr. Hansen had free janitorial service. As he would often remind us, "you kids can have all the spilled feed you can sweep up, so long as you clean that floor at least once a week. I don't want to have to do the work just because you didn't come around often enough." So come around we did, to sweep up the spilled powder.

After a half-century of intervening years, it's certainly overdue (and definitely somewhat conscience soothing) to finally admit publicly to something that Gary and I did at a time when we weren't getting enough of this free food to keep our pigs adequately fed. I'm still mildly ashamed of the misdeed that I'm about to describe, but we were desperate kids back then, and in the greater scheme of life's happenings, at least as viewed in hindsight, no one was hurt. So, here's a very tardy explanation with apology.

Howard Brown was a feedmill customer who transported his grain in a horse-drawn wagon. He owned a team of handsomely matched workhorses. Anyone who has been around such a team knows how very responsive these animals are to voice commands. Well, while farmer Brown chatted with Mr. Hansen near the offloading chute, Gary (or was it me, or perhaps both of us in unison?) ordered the team forward as ground feed was falling into farmer Brown's wagon.

"Cluck, cluck, cluck. Hey, giddyup."

A yard-tall conical mound of the white powder spilled onto the concrete floor about as fast as we could say "Whoa," followed by "Back, back, back. Whoa." Farmer Brown didn't notice the unusually large amount of spillage as he mounted his wagon and urged his team forward. Gary and I certainly did, though, and quickly filled four one-hundred-pound flour sacks with the white powder of ground oats before our ruse could be discovered.

We're sorry, farmer Brown, and want to apologize, from wherever you may be watching us today.

As the summer weeks passed, the arrival of corn-picking season added a new source of food to the pigs' menu. Once again, Gary and I were janitors, this time cleaning up after corn-harvesting machines. With the permission of farmers, we walked cornfield after cornfield collecting full ripe ears that even the most efficient of machines had missed. I can't tell you exactly how many gunnysacks of corn we collected this way, but I remember clearly that we got a ton of physical exercise in the process, if indeed exercise can be measured in tons.

Pigs love corn. They ate our gleanings as fast as we could bring them in. I'm pretty sure that we salvaged *more* than a ton of corn, which can definitely be measured by weight!

By November our pigs looked ready for market. They were certainly big enough to interest Arnold Kaus and his son Gerry, who ran the local livestock-buying company. Besides, Gary and I were back in school, with barely enough free time to keep the pigs in adequate food. With only minor lumps in our throats (we liked those pigs, but the kaching-kaching-kaching of ringing up a profit was a stronger pull on our emotions), we drove the pigs along town streets to the Kaus place of business at the west edge of BV. Though I didn't see or hear her as we herded the pigs away from their pen, I suspect that Patti Paulsen went into fits of wild cheering in the background.

Arnold Kaus was a gregarious and affable man who was popular with all the children in town. He never failed to smile and greet kids on the street, and we all responded with a friendly "hello," no matter that he often smelled of the animals of his business. Of course, so did most other people in a small farming community. In the childhood lingo of the time, Mr. Kaus was definitely one of the "good guys." There were a few universally recognized "bad guys" in BV's adult population, too, who need not be mentioned here by name. These were the folks whose homes were to be avoided at Halloween trick-or-treat time, except to soap their windows and overturn their outhouse on that mischief-ridden holiday evening.

Mr. Kaus put our pigs on his scale, one at a time, as Gary and I stood by and waited anxiously for the results.

"Well you novice pig farmers, I think you're going to like what I see here." His index finger was gently tapping a counterweight incrementally outward on the long horizontal bar of his scale, trying to bring that bar down to a steady and precisely level position. Leverage and mechanical advantage were at work. We watched closely as he gave the weight one last nudge before reading the number of pounds. It looked to me like he had pushed the weight way too far, in our favor.

"What do you know! This fine hog weighs in at two hundred thirty-five pounds."

He went through the same steps with our other two pigs, once again giving that extra push at the end, in our favor.

"Old number two here is two hundred forty pounds, and number three is two hundred thirty. You two should be proud of what you've accomplished." He circled around each pig to examine it from various angles, as though he was judging livestock at the annual county fair. Then, with that Arnold Kaus twinkle in his eye, he pronounced that "these porkers look like such healthy well-proportioned critters that I'm going to pay you top-hog price."

At twenty cents a pound…well, you do the math. Mr. Kaus paid us in cash. Neither Gary nor I had ever seen or held so much money at one time before.

We ran home and split the money fifty-fifty, after reimbursing my dad for the trivial cost of milk powder. Dad made this transaction into a lesson about money management.

"I'm not charging you two interest on the loan for milk powder, even though a bank would." Interest would probably have been only five cents or so, but his point was made. And hey, five cents could be five more Dubble Bubble shots for a Musial card!

Dad continued with our lesson in doing business. "If you want to start making records of your finances for future reference, keep in mind that your gross income is what Arnold paid you. Net income is what's left over after you pay me for the powder." Once again, the difference between the two figures wasn't much, but Dad's point was made and acknowledged.

I netted nearly as much as I typically made during six months of delivering newspapers. And raising pigs had been far more enjoyable than trying to pry money from penny-pinching adult customers over whom I had no effective leverage. Gary pocketed his share of net earnings without uttering a word about how this compared with what he usually had to spend. I translated the big grin on his face to mean that he was as satisfied as I was with our first go at business. We left Dad and walked to the pen…our place of business…to bask in our success.

"G a r y!…G a r y!"

Gary's mother was shouting for him to come home for supper. As he was about to turn and leave, I yelled, "Grab my thumbs and pull!"

Hand-written receipt for the sale of our first batch of hogs. The scrawl under the heading "Remarks" is Arnold Kaus's version of bu, which is his short-hand for butcher hogs.

We alternated between playing the role of milk cow and milker for two more of our farmer handshakes and agreed to raise pigs the following summer if Uncle Clare's sows produced more unfed runts.

Gary streaked home for supper, probably feeling a bit like King Midas. A few seconds later, I burst through the back door of our house, sped through the kitchen and climbed the narrow steep steps, two at a time, to the second floor and my bedroom. Trembling with excitement, I began a written record of our pig-raising business. Little did I know then that I would use those notes much later to write about my childhood antics.

5

Wintertime Blues

The winter of 1953/1954 was a cold bridge across a river of rapid change for me. I was on a countdown to become a teenager when spring arrived. Though just a word, somehow saying an age that ends in "teen" sounds far more grown up than any of those one through twelve words.

I was literally growing *up*, too. Now that my legs and their attached feet could reach the brake, clutch, and accelerator pedals, while my eyes simultaneously peered forward through the windshield, Dad taught me to drive the family car...a sleek maroon aerodynamically shaped Lincoln Zephyr powered by a way-cool V-12 engine. A legal driver's license would have to wait another three years, but still there was plenty of driving practice to be had safely on nearly deserted farm roads where any accident was likely to be of the single vehicle variety and not life threatening.

Color it maroon, add a layer of dust and some dents that come with being seventeen years old, and you have an image of the car that I learned to drive in...a 1936 Lincoln Zephyr sedan powered by a V-12 engine capable of moving the rig at ninety miles per hour.

For the first time in my life, I had enough pocket money to see every cowboy movie that came to town, without having to ask Mother or Dad for some cash. The big-screen adventures of Lash LaRue, Roy Rogers, Hopalong Cassidy, Gene Autry, and the Lone Ranger were all within reach of my very own resources.

Before the pig project, Mother had always been understanding about my requests for a movie dole...maybe in part because she got an Almond Joy, her favorite candy bar, as part of our routine movie deal.

"Here's your quarter, Wendy," she would say. "Now don't forget that my sweet tooth is part of our bargain."

She would place the quarter in the palm of my right hand and squeeze it shut as though she feared I would immediately drop the coin. A lost quarter back then was much more of a financial loss than it would be today. Two hours later, I would bring her one of those candy bars following Hollywood's phony yet entertaining rendition of encounters among cowboys, Indians, and rattlesnakes. At fourteen cents per flick and ten cents per candy bar, I profited by a penny with each trip to the Valley Theater...one more chance to score a Stan Musial card. But it was kind of humiliating to have to ask Mother for money, especially since I was almost something "teen" and longing for independence.

With profits from pigs, I also had enough of my own money to slurp sodas and malts, rather than surreptitiously sipping water while sucking a common pine toothpick.

Awash in newfound wealth or not, though, winters can pass excruciatingly slowly for a kid in frigid Minnesota. Hours of daylight are far fewer than during summer months, and having to be in school gobbles up most of the sun-up time. All winter long, I was emptying wastebaskets and sweeping the floors of Duffield Sinclair Service in darkness; those chores were gloomy enough in full sunshine, even beneath a green-and-white truck-size metal sign bearing the image of a smiling Dino the Dinosaur who urged me and other readers to "Drive with Care and Buy Sinclair."

At twelve years old and counting, I was poised to graduate to the seventh grade. Come on autumn of 1954! Grades one through six were housed in the west wing of BV's public school, which sat atop part of the same gravel bar that hid the Browns Valley Man for nine thousand years. I'd be stuck in that west wing through the rest of the current academic year, which might seem like nine thousand years. Grades seven through twelve were in a mirror-image east wing.

An interconnecting gymnasium separated the two wings, like the body of an awkward-looking gigantic duck, wings extended for flight. As a seventh grader, I would be able to rub shoulders with junior and senior boys in the east-wing hallways between classes. I knew that this would make me feel more important than actually being a "big" boy in the west wing whose halls were infested with running and screaming and giggling immature urchins. Had I really been one of them not so many years ago?

The gymnasium was a quonset-style structure, large enough to house a basketball court sandwiched between four rows of tiered bleacher seats on each side. Double entry doors opened onto one end, and a raised stage for school plays and for band and vocal concerts extended beyond the other end of the court. Dark, dank, and gloomy showers and locker rooms were in a basement, down parallel sets of stairs under the stage…boys to the right and girls to the left. The fungi of athlete's foot thrived down there! I carried irritating evidence of this truth with me into my thirties.

Basketball was always the most popular school sport in town, probably in large part because it provided a fun activity during the bleak winter weeks and months. Music also was very popular, because our music teacher, Mr. Stoyke, made it so. He was incredibly enthusiastic and creative. He discovered and developed latent musical talents in students where none had been apparent. In the annals of Mr. Stoyke's many accomplishments, this was the school year that he wrote music and words for the BV Thunderbirds's fight song, a tune I can still sing from memory. On a more somber note, he also composed a musical score that allowed the school choir to sing an emotional rendition of Lincoln's Gettysburg Address. Parents shed a few tears during our public performance of Stoyke's creation, for reasons that baffled us young students, still quite ignorant of Civil War history.

The offsetting enjoyment of practicing basketball skills, singing in the school choir, and playing trumpet in the school band rendered my all-important-but-yucky English class reasonably tolerable. I still hadn't quite discovered how much fun writing and reading can be, though I was subconsciously headed in that direction.

My science teacher Mr. Peterson, an upstanding Scandinavian Lutheran of Wobegon ilk, was a light shining in the darkness of winter. While sporting the semi-sinister grin of an intense (mad?) laboratory scientist, he managed to make class exciting and memorable by performing a variety of fizzy, fetid, and sometimes seemingly magical experiments by mixing chemicals as we students watched in silent wonder, before trying our best to reproduce his results. Maybe the coolest show-and-tell was when he filled a clear pint-sized glass beaker with carbon dioxide from a metal tank…at least he said he did; we couldn't see a darned thing in the beaker…and then poured the contents over the flame of a burning candle. The flame bent slowly away from the invisible extinguishing vapor as if pushed by an unseen hand and was snuffed out within seconds. The experiment seemed like a ridiculously complicated way to put out a candle when a simple puff exhaled between lips would suffice. But Mr. Peterson stressed an additional lesson.

"You kids should remember dat carbon dioxide is denser than da mix of gases dat make up da atmosphere we breathe. Dats why it flowed down over da candle. And, yah shure, if you ever get caught in a closed or low place when dat heavy gas is around, your life candle will be snuffed out." That kind of information can grab the attention of the dullest of students!

The 1953/1954 academic year of my formal education marked the winter when Duane Labs accidentally sliced his thumb off with a table saw in shop class. He'd been so intent on making an accurate cut across a board for a bookshelf construction project that he forgot to move his hand out of harm's way. The rest of us watched in fascinated horror, once Duane's screaming announced the accident. We learned just how powerful Duane's lungs and vocal cords were that day. And most of us decided that the sight of (someone else's!) real blood and gore was very interesting, much more so than the sterile stuff that messed up a lab bench while dissecting a pickled frog in biology class.

Duane's thumb wasn't quite cut off, although it looked ready to drop into a pile of sawdust on the floor beneath the blood-stained saw as it dangled by the thinnest thread of skin and muscle, twisting just enough for the thumb nail to intermittently reflect a flash of light.

"Hey look!" yelled Gary. "Duane's thumb nail is like that spinning ceiling fixture with lots of little mirrors that are supposed to make a romantic atmosphere at the senior prom dance."

As the rest of us students laughed, the teacher frowned at Gary and rushed Duane and his barely attached bleeding stump off for medical attention. Miraculously, that thumb was successfully reattached. When healed enough for use once again as the opposing digit on his right hand, an ugly scar and the story behind it gave Duane a built-in conversation piece that served as an icebreaker for what became an enviably long line of girlfriends. Seeing that kind of magic with the opposite gender, more than one other guy in shop class was tempted to create a similar scar for himself, though no one ever worked up the courage (or foolishness!) to run a finger through the saw.

This was also the year that Butch Lubbers impaled my side with the just-sharpened lead of a 7H pencil as we horsed around in mechanical drawing class. I learned that pointed 7H lead is about as hard, strong, and piercing as the blade of a dime-store pocketknife. The accident left me with a permanent graphite-colored patch where lead penetrated skin, but I couldn't put this body imperfection to use with girls the way Duane did his scar, unless I pulled my shirttail halfway up to my head; teachers properly discouraged that kind of behavior in classrooms, and even in hallways.

The short and cold days dragged on, but eventually December and then Christmas rolled around…a holiday season that was certain to help displace wintertime blues with a red-letter program of student parties, gift exchanges, and family gatherings. With my hard-earned pig money, I could be (and was, I think) unusually generous with the gifts I bought for my five sisters, mother, and dad. That round of spending sure ate into the balance of my net earnings, though, and made me even more anxious for spring and another opportunity to rescue some runty piglets from starvation.

I got to thinking about this situation so much that I wrote a couple of porcine verses to one of the family Christmas songs that filled the piano room of our house each year. I suppose I was too shy and embarrassed to share my verses with the family back then, but it seems okay to go public now.

Dad's mother (Nina Hatchitt Duffield), who died at such a young age that I never got to meet her, had somehow found time to write songs, poems, and essays while raising a family of five sons and a daughter on a farm northeast of town, a few miles outside the valley of River Warren. The family remembered Grandma Duffield each Christmas by singing some of her compositions. One song in particular was the favorite of my dad and his brothers, because there was a separate verse that had been written for each of them…that is, for each of the four oldest boys. At the time Grandma Duffield wrote the song, her youngest two offspring had not yet been born; special verses for these babies had never been added.

As was the family's custom, the Duffields gathered at our house on Christmas Day. An otherwise tasty meal featured last year's rock-hard fruitcake for dessert, an offering that would be passed around the table and reappear whole for years to come. When the ladies had finished washing and drying dishes, Dad got the Duffield choir organized. "Attention everyone! It's time for the music." We all migrated to the piano.

My aunt Fonty, the youngest of Dad's siblings, sidled her bottom side back and forth on the piano bench until she was comfortable and began playing the musical score of "Hurry Up Old Santa Claus." Everyone knew the words by heart. We sang all the verses together, rather than letting an awkwardly sad silence remind us that the son for whom the fourth verse had been written never returned from the European theater of World War II. Voices covered the range from bass to soprano to childish squeaky. The sound of our impromptu choir was remarkably pleasant, considering the fact that no one had had formal voice training. Singing began with a spirited rendition of the chorus,

Hurry up, old Santa Claus.
We can't be good much longer.
Hurry up, old Santa Claus.
We can't be good much longer.

followed by the usual sequence of verses.

ALL

December is the longest month.
With this you'll all agree.
For just before old Santa comes,
We're good as we can be. (Chorus)

FIRST SON

This week I split up cords of wood,
Which no one seemed to see.
I'll tell you what, this bein' good
Is mighty hard on me! (Chorus)

SECOND SON

I milked the Jersey good an' dry,
And that's an awful chore.
I did my best and I don't see why
She kicked me out the door! (Chorus)

THIRD SON

I walked a mile to get the mail,
And brought it in a sack.
And all my mamma said to me:
"Why didn't you hurry back?" (Chorus)

FOURTH SON

I put my playthings on the shelf.
That's high up on the wall.
And when I fell and hurt myself,
I did not cry at all! (Chorus)

ALL

Now, at our house on Christmas Day
There's bound to be a riot.
And then our dad is sure to say:
"Why can't you kids be quiet!" (Chorus)

While the rest of the family reorganized to sing another tune by Grandma Duffield, I silently hummed my verses, written in hopes and anticipation of raising another batch of piglets. I'd penned my words in the privacy of my bedroom during the preceding few weeks, knowing there would be the annual family sing-along at Christmas.

CHORUS

Hurry up pig birthing season.
Produce a few more runts.
Hurry up pig birthing season.
We'll watch as income mounts.

VERSE ONE

We raised three piglets all by hand.
We did just fine, I'll gloat.
And our reward at market time
Was not one more pine float. (Chorus)

VERSE TWO

We watched as piglets grew to hogs
On hand-scrounged corn and feed.
When fall and market day rolled 'round
Our net was good indeed. (Chorus)

The messages conveyed by my verses rang rather crassly commercial, compared to the wholesome family-life thoughts expressed by Grandma Duffield's
lines. But then, the pig project had put money in my pocket while keeping me
busy at something other than marking, or just plain wasting time during the
summer months. So, maybe my verses weren't too far out of line with some part
of the Christmas spirit, after all. I supposed the content didn't matter much anyway, since I was the only one who knew those verses existed. Not even Gary knew
about them. They were the stuff of secret diary notes.

With Christmas and New Year's Eve behind us, January and February passed
slowly through many days when the daytime temperature never rose above zero.
Canadian Arctic air masses often came to visit BV. The coal-fired boiler at school
could barely keep up with demand for hot water to circulate through radiators.
We students left our cold wooden seats and huddled around radiators whenever
teachers permitted. At home, our family formed a semi-circle in front of a small
kerosene-burning Unger stove, which sat in a corner of the largest room on the
ground floor. Unger provided the only heat for our poorly insulated Victorian
house of 1900 vintage. A few of the Unger-generated calories found their way to
the second-story bedrooms by rising convectively through small metal-grate-cov-
ered openings between the two floors. You can be sure that my sisters and I
wasted no time during the clothes off, pajamas on routine on the way to diving
beneath a thick pile of blankets at night. About ten seconds was all I needed to
get between wintertime flannel sheets.

Unger's calories notwithstanding, water pipes could freeze overnight, forcing Dad to fire up a blowtorch and squeeze into narrow awkward spaces to heat the pipes. His contortions sometimes led to loud and unusual words, which tasteful authors represent with such symbols as ✱ ✗ # ✳ 🗯 ! ✻. We kids were not supposed to hear those words, in spite of a volume that may have carried to neighboring houses!

Bright sunshine on days when the outdoor temperature rose above zero enticed us to play outside on weekends. Abundant snowfall provided excellent sledding and amateurish attempts at skiing on the hills bounding River Warren's valley. Flat-ground fun relied on cars and horses, instead of gravity, for the force needed to move sleds, toboggans, and skiers across snowy ground.

In "How Angel Peterson Got His Name," Gary Paulsen writes that this grow-ing-up buddy of his set a new speed record on skis while being towed by a '39 Ford sedan. The only record I dare claim while being towed on skis at BV is suc-cessfully swerving quickly enough to avoid a face splattered with the sticky fresh droppings of the horse pulling me…perhaps not so nerve-wracking as Angel Peterson's seventy-five-miles-per-hour experience, but still unusual enough to qualify as an extreme sport.

During nearly four of the winter months, Traverse and Big Stone were sealed with two to three feet of ice. Snow-free patches were popular skating rinks for kids and adults alike. Stoically tough individuals (most with names ending in "son," reflecting a Scandinavian heritage that seems imbued with a natural resis-tance to frigid weather) braved the cold to fish at holes chopped through the ice. Some of these thick-skinned "sons" sat for hours on stools in the wind-swept open while others were sheltered in the relative warmth of unheated sheds. I could never understand why anyone would submit himself to such discomfort, especially since I was not fond of the taste of fish.

Commercial fishermen opened holes through the ice large enough to deploy nets for snaring hundreds of carp per pull. Though most people I've told about the main product of this business have been dubious, freshly smoked carp is quite tasty…if you like the taste of fish at all. Some of the fish were trucked live hun-dreds of miles to markets along the Gulf of Mexico coast. There was sufficient demand for that bottom-feeding trash fish to provide a profitable, albeit small, industry for wintertime BV.

Adults and kids old enough to drive used the frozen lakes as safe surfaces for practicing the four-wheeled version of ice-skating. Everyone growing up in a BV type of winter environment knew that a car purposely spinning and twirling completely out of control on a huge sheet of ice is preferable to accidentally being caught in the same gyrations at a busy intersection. Safe car skating is exhilarating! Duane Labs of the nearly severed thumb is said to have maneuvered his dark green 1937 Chevy coupe into four consecutive clockwise spins before sliding to a halt ten feet from a patch of open water. That cat of a guy seemed to use another of his proverbial nine lives at least twice each year!

Come the first hint of spring, politicians of BV's town government sold lottery tickets for an annual fundraiser. At a dollar per guess, you could try to predict the date, hour, and minute that a discarded household appliance would break through thawing ice and sink to the bottom of Traverse. During my growing-up years, I thought this custom was cute, neat, fun…you name it. Ancient appliances went down into the watery depths like enemies forced off Captain Hook's gangplank. Only later did I come to understand that littering a lake bottom with old washers, driers, fridges, and freezers was not a proper way to sustain the integrity of a body of water. Those machines may have created new habitat for a few carp and other bottom dwellers, but I think there must have been plenty of natural habitat to accommodate Traverse fish!

Hints of spring also started to melt back several-feet-thick accumulations of snow that preserved a stratified record, in the style of Grand Canyon rock layering, of each blizzard that had hit the area during the winter season. Layer upon layer of snow, here and there separated by the dark layers of wind-blown Great Plains dust, bespoke of temperatures that had never risen above freezing for nearly four months. Brrrrrr!! Yah shure, in the Scandinavian accent, dis accumulated snow layering was baby stuff compared to da mile-thick package of horizontal rocks exposed in da walls of Arizona's famous canyon. And, yah shure, only four months of a snowy record pale next to da hundreds of millions of years represented by Grand Canyon rocks. But as our BV science teacher Mr. Peterson might have told his neighbor, "Ya know, Ole, snow and ice are rocks, too. They yust happen to melt at a ridiculously low temperature compared to solid old sandstone and granite. If ya want to be remembered long after death, ya won't be orderin' a headstone made of ice rock now, will ya."

Gary and I did our part to enjoy winter activities and endure homework, but mostly we were anxious for spring to arrive. March blew in, providing the annual season of kite flying. The point of sunrise on the eastern horizon continued its northward advance. Orion disappeared from the nighttime sky. Snow melted faster, as longer and warmer daylight hours nudged aside the cold dark depths of winter. Our playful melt-water channeling probably once again moved the continental divide in BV a bit north or south.

April brought squeals of delight from Gary and me as squeals of 1954's crop of piglets announced new life in Uncle Clare's birthing shed.

6

It Took A Village

Uncle Clare knew that Gary and I were lurking around that shed…waiting to see if runts in need of rescuing would appear in this year's crop of piglets. It seemed that practically the whole town knew the main thought that was racing around in our minds. We visited the birthing shed regularly, hoping to see litters where piglets outnumbered teats by a large enough factor for a baby or two to fail in the fight for mother's milk. As fate would have it, four of those skin-and-bone weaklings came our way. Once again, Uncle Clare's Duroc sows demonstrated how very successful they were at making babies.

"We've got our work cut out for us this year," Gary understated as he and I tried to digest the enormity of raising four instead of three piglets. We were in the garage pouring a newly mixed batch of milk into a feeding pan. I nodded my head in silent agreement and wondered if I deserved to keep wearing the farmer's uniform of bib overalls. We were up against an awesome challenge. But we weren't about to give up.

We were also destined to play out a test of the "bigger" word of the French belief about the American psyche. At fall market time, we would discover whether or not "bigger" would lead to "better" for our pig-raising project. Meanwhile, we definitely needed more and bigger of just about everything involved in the project.

Having four piglets created the need for more pen space, though not immediately. Four made for a crowded cardboard house, but early on *Piglet Palace* provided warm early spring shelter for the runts, before the combined weight of their bodies, huddled beneath the heat lamp and pushing against weak walls, provided enough force to burst a seam. Patch-all duct tape healed the house.

About three weeks later, and not by accident I imagine, Uncle Clare came calling to see how our project was coping for space at the very moment that another seam looked about to tear open across the bold print of Kenmore Refrigerator.

"I've got a fenced-in piece of land," he began, "where you two could pen your growing pigs. It's at the south end of one of my cornfields, on the valley floor just down below the birthing shed. There's plenty of space there for four pigs."

Gary and I shared a "sigh-of-relief" glance. "Thanks, Uncle Clare," I gushed, giving our glance expression. "We really need a place like that." Somehow I'd known that Uncle Clare would bail us out of the space problem. He was about the best uncle a kid could want.

As it turned out, Uncle Clare was only the first of a number of people in BV who would help Gary and me through our growing pains. We hadn't been aware of what the local buzz was as we raised our first batch of piglets, but we learned later that our project had become "the talk of the town." Well, not so much *the* talk as the weather always is in a farming community. But as Dad mentioned on the day that we divvied up that first batch of pig money, "Lots of folks around town think you two are quite the young businessmen and farmers. I overheard compliments in conversations at several stores along Main Street this summer, even from Merv Zabel at the bank where he's working toward taking over that business. If *he* can say nice things about what you two have accomplished, after his step-in-the-poop accident, I think most of the town is behind you."

Dad was dead-on right. The amount of real and moral support we had enjoyed last year with space, feed, and marketing would increase enough to make the second year of our project even more successful than the first. Throughout that summer of 1954 and on into fall, we experienced the BV version of a concept popularized by the phrase, "It Takes a Village," the idea being that community efforts towards laudable goals lead to enriching results for all humanity. Whew! This explanation sounds awfully complicated and stuffy for the simple fact that good happens when people help each other.

As far as Gary and I were concerned, Uncle Clare was an A-1 member of the village. He'd known that we were going to need a large pen to hold our flock of four, and he helped find...naw, that's way too weak...he *provided* the solution.

Of course, an unspoken reason for needing a different pen for that four-pig year was as obvious as the nose on Patti Paulsen's face. If she had been so unhappy with three pigs living across the street, surely she would finally formally object if even more oinking, pooping porkers were within sight, sound, and sometimes smelling distance.

When we moved our rapidly growing pigs to Uncle Clare's out-of-town place, they were only a ten-minute walk from home yet far enough downwind to avoid offending even the most sensitive nostrils of a BV citizen.

As an added benefit to Patti's love life, Merv Zabel's spiffy loafers would never again become sullied because of an errant misstep when he came to collect her, although there were plenty of family-pet dogs that roamed our neighborhood and these animals were not famous for their fastidious bathroom habits.

"Food. We've got to figure out a way to get our hands on more free food this year, if we're gonna make a profit. When the piglets need solid food, we won't be able to sweep up enough ground feed for them...unless we pull another trick on Howard Brown," I added with a slight chuckle in my voice.

Whether out of fear of being caught, guilt and remorse at what we'd done earlier, or some other strong emotions, we would never again *create* spillage at the feedmill. But we still liked to brag about what we'd done, though only to ourselves.

"And the corn-pickin' season comes too late to fill in for ground feed."

I was thinking out loud as Gary and I watched four hungry critters suck up their milk about as fast as we could pour it into their dish, a mixing bowl borrowed from Mother's kitchen. If our efforts had been stretched thin to gather enough to feed our three pigs last year, how could we possibly gather enough for four hungry animals this year?

Part of our solution to the lean food supply came by gathering food in advance of need. We began to clean the feedmill floor as soon as we knew how many mouths we had to feed. By the time solid food was needed, we had several hundred-pound sacks of ground feed stored in the garage, without seriously considering a repeat of the prank with Howard Brown's well-trained team of draft horses. We simply took, with much vocal gratitude, what was offered.

"Thanks, Mr. Hansen," we said each visit to his feedmill. "Thanks a lot for letting us clean up the spilled feed at your mill."

"You're welcome boys," he would reply. "Just be sure to keep that floor clean."

On the heels of a late summer harvest, we walked many miles through cornfields, gathering in the ears missed by machines. We stole dinner from many a frightened, angry, outspoken, and still-hungry ring-necked pheasant and Canada goose as we played the role of gleaners. But in spite of all our food-gathering efforts, sometime between depleting the inventory of the early gathered ground feed and the onset of corn harvest, we lacked adequate food for the pigs. This is when help from many people of our village gave solid meaning to the aphorism "waste not, want not." We put a marginal resource to productive use.

Unlike people, who can be quite persnickety about what they devour, pigs will eat all manner of vegetable matter. As the word-of-mouth message about our food shortage circulated around town, table scraps that would normally have found their way to the city dump became yet another source of food for our pigs.

Pounds and piles of orts, those table leftovers that people seem to find distasteful, or at least unwanted, saved our bacon in a figure of speech, while adding more bacon-on-the-hoofs of the four pigs.

Speaking of bacon: I have no bone to pick with vegetarians, assuming they would deign to join in picking at something that once carried meat; some of my best friends are vegetarians. But isn't it a little bit sad that they never taste the remarkable result of vegetable stuff (otherwise destined to ferment and molder in a garbage pit) transformed into tender, mouthwatering pork?

Come market time, Arnold Kaus was once again our village prince. Gary and I watched as he gave the scale's counterweight an extra nudge, in our favor, for each of the four pigs.

"Well my young friends," he announced, "this year you've raised six hundred ninety pounds of market hogs. You're turning into quite the townie farmers."

Once again, he paid us top-hog price, when in fact our pigs were rather ordinary specimens. Two were almost too small to qualify for market hogs. I think Mr. Kaus called them market hogs simply out of kindness to us. The per-pound price had held almost steady during the past year. You can do the math, but I swear on my childhood collection of favorite shiny rocks that Gary and I were once again walking around with what seemed to us like a fortune in our bib-over-all pockets. Seeing how giddy we were in experiencing such wealth, Mr. Kaus cautioned, "Now you kids take that cash right home, divide it up, and each of you put your share in a safe place."

We hoped he heard us shouting "yes, sir," as we ran toward home, half-hitched overall bibs a-flapping. With a detour to Gettman's Red Owl store, we used two cents of our new wealth for Dubble Bubble.

"Dang! Another Jimmie Piersall. What about you?"

"I got a stupid Rizzuto. That makes three," moaned Gary. Musial was still elusive.

At Dad's suggestion and urging, I went to the bank the next day to open a savings account with my share of the net profit. Union State, BV's only bank, was one of a couple dozen places of business that lined Main Street. Having never before been to that building, I was overwhelmed by the thick-and-massive granite facade, and the atmosphere of seriously quiet business, once inside. The adult customers were speaking in whispers as though they wanted their financial dealings kept secret. The place was as noise-free as Mr. Beaulieu's funeral home during a visitation period. This was not an environment for fun and frivolity. Even a sneeze would seem unwelcome. This was the kind of setting you might expect to be ejected from for something as innocent as laughter. It was definitely not a place to be popping pink bubbles.

BROWNS VALLEY, MINN.
PHONE 47

CHOKIO, MINN.
PHONE 70

ARNOLD & GERRY KAUS

Nº 15395

12/2 19 54

Bought of _Gardner & Duffield_

Address _B. V. Minn._

Remarks	Hogs				WEIGHT	Price	AMOUNT
Fin	1				210.	17 00	35 70
						17—	
Other	2				220	17 00	37 40
Lea	1				260	16—	41 60
							114 70
HAULING							

Paid by_____

Check No. _____

Amount_____ Rec'd. by_____

CALL US BEFORE SELLING YOUR LIVESTOCK

THE VALLEY NEWS PUBLISHING CO., BROWNS VALLEY, MINN.

Hand-written receipt for the sale of our second batch of hogs. Two of the four weighed so little (220 pounds total) that they carried the label ltbu (light butcher hogs). Mr. Kaus did the long division for us, to show how to split the money fifty-fifty.

I raised a clenched right hand to my mouth and faked a stifled cough. The Dubble Bubble wad ended up in my fist. The fist went into my hip pocket where a red farmer's handkerchief (for wiping dirty things clean, not blowing one's nose!) made a perfect holding wrap for the wad. Mother wouldn't be happy about sticky gum in the kerchief, but better that than the pocket lining of the overalls.

Temptation to blow a bubble gone, I walked across the lone rectangular business room to face one of three openings along a steel-bar wall that extended to the ceiling from atop a counter that spanned from wall to wall. I stood on tiptoes for a clear view over the counter. No clerk was in sight. Straight back I saw a sturdy-looking flat gray wall interrupted only by a massive steel walk-through door that must have led to where the bank's treasure was kept…at least that's how banks were set up in cowboy movies. "Hah!" I muttered silently. I knew from silver-screen examples that massive steel notwithstanding, any Saturday matinee cowboy crook could break into this kind of vault…maybe by using a stick of dynamite, or maybe by having his horse pull on a rope tied to the door. But why bother? Roy Rogers or another of the good guy heroes would catch the thief before he could cross the county line.

Back to reality, I broke a sticky sweat when I saw Mr. Zabel appear from nowhere (a secret room behind the counter?) and approach to wait on me. He was wearing a dark suit with matching vest. His tie was similarly dark, as was what thin and receding hair decorated his balding pate. Vertical slats of stark starched white shirt peeked out between tie and vest. He spread his open hands palms down across the counter, peered down at me through horn-rimmed glasses, and smiled. "Well, well. Hello, W e n d y," he said, drawing out the pronunciation enough to make me silently cringe more than usual at the sound of my nickname.

"Hello, Mr. Zabel," I began tentatively. "I uh…I have some money here that I want to use to open a savings account. My dad thinks it would be a good idea." I dug deeply into my pockets, extracted an unsorted mish-mash of coins and cash, and reached up to pile it on the counter.

He watched me in silent amusement, and then quickly rearranged the pile with the eraser end of a pencil. "Here, young man. You'll need these more than the bank will," he said, pushing two nails, a loop of wire, a strand of baling twine, and a shiny pea-size red-and-white banded agate back toward me. He immediately began to sort and count the rest of my offering…paper to his right and coin to his left. I watched intently, hoping he wouldn't try to palm a bill or two the way a shady poker player had at the Stagecoach Saloon in last Saturday's movie.

As I watched my money on the move, I noticed that Mr. Zabel had the cleanest, softest-looking and palest hands I'd ever seen on a BV man. His fingernails were the color of pure ivory and flawless in appearance. The adult male hands in town that I was familiar with were heavily callused, deeply stained from the materials they handled, and tipped with chewed-on split stubs of nails. Some of these rough hands were also scarred, and a few were disfigured by missing digits that had been plucked, chewed up, and spit out by one uncaring machine or another. Even I was developing the used hands of a fledgling farmer. Counting money apparently didn't qualify as manual labor.

My reverie on what hands say about one's work was interrupted when Mr. Zabel stopped counting at an even one hundred dollars. He cleared his throat with a grrrrnn. "How nice to see a young man ready to recognize the importance of banking, to save for a rainy day. Your father is a wise man." I felt like that rainy day was now, as droplets of sweat gathered to skitter down the cleft of my back like a channeled cloudburst inside my bib overalls. Still, my introduction to banking proceeded smoothly enough, despite my uneasiness. Mr. Zabel continued his count. He was down to the small stuff.

"One hundred sixty, one sixty one, one sixty two, one sixty three, one sixty four...and eighty four cents." He finished his tally, having created order from chaos, in full view on the counter between us. Thank goodness his total agreed with mine. "This is quite a tidy sum for a youngster to have accumulated. It seems that the pig project is quite successful."

"Yes sir. And there's some paper route money in there, too," I explained.

During the following five decades, my experience with bankers has been that their facial expressions are difficult to interpret. Smiles are the rule, but I've learned from more than one experience that not all friendly looking banker smiles are truly friendly. Whatever feelings were behind his expression that day, Mr. Zabel looked pleased as he added my money to carefully organized bill-and-coin-sized compartments in a drawer he had opened behind the counter. He handed me a receipt and a ledger showing an entry of $164.84. He nodded to indicate that our business transaction was complete.

I was puzzled. Was this really how it worked? I expected more...but what more I didn't know. I had entrusted Mr. Zabel with my entire cash savings, and all I got in return was a piece of paper saying that I had that much money in the bank. As a first timer, I wondered if Mr. Zabel would give the money back right now if I asked for it. That meager piece of paper in my hand represented a level of trust that was new to me. What if my sweaty palms blurred the numbers on that paper? Who, then, would know how much of the money in the back-wall vault was mine? His voice interrupted my silent, though perhaps apparent worrying.

"Remember young man, your money is safe with us and will earn dividends every day that it's here in the bank. We're currently paying one point two five percent annual interest. You can watch your savings grow with each statement we mail you." I heard a "Good day, now. Please greet your father for me," as he turned and disappeared back into the mystery space behind the counter.

I turned and shuffled out through the entry door, quietly, in keeping with bank decorum. I exhaled deeply and leaned against the granite wall outside, squashing the wad of Dubble Bubble flat as I wondered about the safety of my life savings. For reasons unknown to me then, all that money would vanish within a couple of years, but not because of any shenanigans by Mr. Zabel and the bank. Meanwhile, he was right, of course. I watched my savings grow with each monthly statement. But I wasn't very impressed. One point two five percent of $164.84 is.... You do the math to test your level of being impressed.

Paltry increments of interest notwithstanding, having money in the bank got me to thinking about the Harley Davidson motorcycle I wanted to buy as soon as I could safely ride one. I already had a Cushman scooter...a motorized two-wheeler powerful enough to carry Gary and me with a sack full of corn or ground feed astraddle the bench-seat under us. Dad had earlier agreed that he and I would shop for a used Harley, once I was big enough to handle something that tall and heavy. Given where the money to do this was coming from, it was extra cool that the popular name for a Harley was a Hog.

My friend Darrel Spinler already had one. He let me sit on it to get the feel of being a Harley man. My legs could touch the ground for balance at a standstill, but I knew I would never be able to get his bulky Harley upright if ever it tipped on its side. Of course, Darrel couldn't either, and he was two years older and a lot stronger than me.

To stay upright, a biker needed excellent hand-and-foot coordination with an old Harley. The clutch was operated with a foot pedal, and shifting of gears was done with a hand-operated knob mounted on the side of the gas tank, which left only one hand on the steering bar at critical gear-changing times. Darrell had the needed coordination. He was one of BV's best basketball players.

Darrel took me for rides now and then; wind blowing through my hair in a background of rumble and vibration from a twin-cylinder V-engine gave me hard-to-explain feelings of freedom and exhilaration. I had to have one of those machines, the sooner the better. Two more years of raising pigs might net enough money for a used Harley, and then I could get my driver's license, too.

◆   ◆   ◆

Our pig-raising project during the summer of 1955 was a near clone of 1954. Once again we began with four Duroc runts. To the continued delight of the courting couple Patti and Merv, we reused the pen at the downwind east edge of town. We played the role of hard-working gleaners, and with some community orts thrown into the mix of ground feed and corn on the cob, we were able to produce seven hundred fifty pounds of market hog on the hoof. At weighing and hog-flesh-grading time, Mr. Kaus was his usual generous self. My savings account increased by seventy dollars that autumn. But I still had a steep net-profit hill to climb if I were to afford a Harley, even a used bike, anytime soon.

Fantasizing about the Harley spawned an idea of how Gary and I might be able to have a significantly bigger animal-raising project, but without any additional work on our part. Though extra effort had been involved compared to year one, bigger measured by number of pigs had been only marginally better during the second and third years of the project...if net profit is the measure of better. To invigorate that track record, I had a plan for diversification to create enough additional profit the coming year to put a Harley within financial reach by the time a driver's license was tucked proudly into my billfold...right next to a "secret" photo of Lois Westbrock.

As an aging fourteen year old, yucky had turned to maybe yummy in my outlook toward the opposite gender. The times they were a changin'.

I had the coming winter to think through my new plan, to test it in my mind from different angles, before talking with Uncle Clare about the role he and his runty baby animals would play. Sometime during the winter doldrums I'd run the idea past Gary to see if he agreed that we could increase net profit without working any harder.

Meanwhile, I could enjoy plenty of movies at the Valley Theater and tasty teenager food at Agar's Cafe. Asking for yet another of Mother's quarters and sipping pine floats were indignities of the past.

Gary and I were buying several pieces of Dubble Bubble each day with our earnings, but owning the Musial card was still only a wish. Our jaw muscles were growing faster than our baseball card collections.

*I'm starting to ponder a plan of animal-raising diversification to make
money for buying a Harley Davidson.*

7

The Bissell Epistle

Do you remember how some days of your childhood turned out the opposite of what you expected them to be? Well, maybe not exactly the opposite, but for sure something happened that you could never have imagined might take place…or even be possible. When something like this hits, it's an unanticipated kick to one's feelings of comfortable familiarity. The surprise might be pleasant or not…a little like dreams.

I'd had lots of dreams by the time I was fourteen, and not one of them had come true. When the pig project got underway, I started dreaming about being at the controls of a bright-red bellowing Harley with increasing frequency. Because Dad was in my corner, I was pretty sure that *that* dream would soon become a reality, if only Gary and I could keep the project going.

It was late autumn. I was at my desk gazing dreamily through a cracked window, barely hearing the teacher's words about various mathematical manipulations. In the battle of the seasons, winter was already tugging away at autumn, trying to get an early start. The first snow of the 1955/1956 version of Minnesota's annual ice age was drifting down from a slate gray sky. Individual flakes were platters. Each delicately and uniquely shaped six-sided flat crystal caught enough air during free fall to stay suspended, like an earth-bound autumn leaf, as though it didn't want to touch the ground. Touching meant instant death by melting, because residual summer heat stored in the soil had not yet been displaced by winter's approaching chill.

The glass I was looking through was so old that it physically sagged with its years, as did the old school building's roofs and floors. More than sixty-five years old, all structural parts of the building suffered the fate of an aging athlete whose once tightly toned biceps, abs, and pecs drooped from a force as weak as gravity-induced tug. The sagging glass distorted my view of the snow-dance scene.

Outdoor temperature was barely below freezing. The large white flakes stuck to chilled leafless branches of box elder trees that lined the street along the front of the school. It was only October. Such an early snowstorm might portend an extra-harsh winter.

Harsh winter or not, a stormy event that would soon start to stick to and pile up on me would be something that no one in our family or in all of BV could have anticipated…one of those complete surprises that are said to fall out of the blue, rather than from a gray sky. As destiny (or perhaps random chance?) would have it, the path of my life was about to experience a bend as abrupt as those forming in the box elder branches increasingly stressed by the accumulating weight of October snow.

Most of my winter that year, though, was what we children of the rural Upper Midwest considered to be normal. Once the last autumn leaf had fallen and early morning lawns were regularly coated with a shimmering white rind of frost, summer clothes were stuffed into the back corners of closets. Wool socks, snow boots, sweaters, parkas, long underwear, mittens, and thickly insulated hats moved up front. Concerned mothers instructed their children to tuck ears flat behind earmuffs, or suffer the humiliation of permanently protruding sound-catching appendages later in life. Properly dressed, we found ways to have weekend fun in the snow and on the frozen lakes, as an antidote to classroom time plus homework, homework, and more homework.

No one mangled a thumb or any other digit with the table saw in shop class that year. Duane continued to do a show-and-tell performance with the two-year-old scar across his right thumb for any member of the opposite gender who would pay attention. But this girl attractor was becoming passé. It was no longer a novelty. So Duane, being very much a fun-loving Duane, created a new technique to catch the attention of the fairer sex. This time a thumb-like appendage was put to such unconventional use that he sent shock waves throughout the BV school, if not the entire town.

To explain, I have to take you on a virtual tour of the communal shower of the boys' locker room, beneath the stage at the end of the basketball court. To borrow a word from a John Irving novel, it was patently obvious to all who showered there with fellow students that Duane had an unusually large flaccid *doink*. This fact was macho-boy talk of the locker room set. As an old saying goes, "if you've got it, flaunt it." Duane playfully flaunted his seemingly oversized thing by cutting a hole in the pocket lining of a pair of his blue jeans, through which he threaded that *doink* when teenage mischief was on his mind.

Now, close your eyes and visualize Duane balanced precariously on a step ladder, stretching to hold the end of a long crepe paper streamer against the basketball backboard, where it needed to be taped as a decoration for the homecoming dance. "Dorothy," he called. Or was it Marlys or Bonnie or Janet? "Come here and gimme a hand, would ya." Even five decades after the fact, I can vividly imagine Duane's giddy and growing feeling of "gotcha" as the classmate joined him at the ladder. "Could ya reach into my right front pocket and pass me the role of tape that's in there?"

Who could refuse such a reasonable call for help from an over-extended classmate? Whoever that female was probably wished she had refused once she realized that her fingers wrapped around a soft and warm *doink*, rather than a cool firm plastic tape dispenser. Rumor has it that she let out a scream heard all around the town.

School principal Bambenek and superintendent Shelver were not entertained by Duane's prank. On the other hand, this was a first-class example of macho-boy behavior whose legend would be passed down from generation to generation.

On a more mundane note, Butch Lubbers didn't accidentally stab me with another sharp 7H pencil that year, in spite of our continued horsing around in mechanical drawing.

There *was* a memorable accident at school, though, the day that one of the Hanson brothers broke both arms simultaneously when he jumped from the auditorium stage and splatted down clumsily on the hard tile of the basketball floor. I think he was trying to get the attention of a cute girl. If so, he did. The attention of everyone in the area was riveted on him as he got up from the floor and held his forearms horizontally, out front.

"Hey look at me," he shouted, apparently feeling no pain...yet. About half-way between wrist and elbow, both arms were splayed out at unnatural angles. Together they mimicked the shape of the forked sides of a slingshot made from a carefully selected willow branch, or the diverging ends of a bizarre-looking Y-shaped metal tool that Steve Morse, BV's most successful driller, used to witch for water-well sites.

Young master Hanson didn't play any football or basketball that year, and for several weeks he looked downright clumsy and silly walking around with heavy twin white casts covering his arms from wrist to elbow. He got just about every student in school to autograph one cast or the other; there was plenty of surface area. Amused teachers signed, too...save one.

Instead, our athletics coach assembled the male student body for a brief to-the-point lecture about how to avoid such limb-breaking accidents. "Don't go jumping onto hard surfaces from such dumb heights," he said loudly, staring us down to be sure that we were listening and got his point. He was understandably concerned about student well being, and also upset about how competitive his teams would be. The BV Thunderbirds were in an athletic conference of such sparsely populated school districts that the starting lineup of a football team consisted of only eight players; a conventional eleven-man team would lack adequate substitutes. With so few potential athletes, the absence of just one or two guys could put a serious crimp in the quality of any starting sports lineup.

That coach, the one-and-only for all sports, was also the English teacher...Marlowe Severson. Adults called him Red, a nickname whose choice was as obvious as the carpet of red hair that covered his head. Every time I heard that cool nickname, I hated my Wendy moniker even more.

As is too often true of immature fun-loving students, who tend to think about the rest of the day or maybe the next hour rather than the longer term, English was not a particularly popular class in our school. In hindsight, though, it should have been. I assure you that Mr. Severson was an excellent instructor who taught English with techniques whose results almost certainly made long-term beneficial impacts on the lives of many of his students. He was unusually talented, demanding, and successful for faculty at a small and rather isolated school district like that of BV.

He assigned books to read and required a multi-page hand-written report from each student on what was understood to be the central message. He taught us to recognize the various parts of speech (nouns, pronouns, verbs, adverbs, adjectives, conjunctions, prepositions, interjections) and how to diagram sentences as a way to understand how words form a systematic structure to create them. He made us put this knowledge to use at the beginning of each class by writing a topic sentence on the blackboard and then instructing us to spend the next fifteen minutes composing an essay on that topic.

He would stride into the room precisely at the scheduled class-starting time. "Okay, students," he would say. "Today's topic is *Honesty is the best policy.*" He continued to talk as he wrote this on the blackboard. "You have the usual fifteen minutes to write something grammatically correct and convincing. You may disagree with the message of the topic sentence, but if so, you must develop logical arguments for your position."

Mr. Severson always returned graded essays the following day, and invited us students to talk with him about them if we had questions. His grading included comments aimed at improving grammar, logic, and penmanship, in contrast to "lazy" teachers who simply wrote a letter grade on an exam paper without an explanation of how the grade was determined.

That winter of 1955/1956 saw our pig-raising project enter the English classroom. As a way to help students learn to be public speakers, Mr. Severson had teams of students enact interviews on various topics. Gary was assigned to inter-view me about what was involved with raising pigs. In a pseudo sound-studio set-ting, he sat in the chair behind Mr. Severson's desk at the front of the classroom, while I was positioned off to the side on a stool. The general idea was that our words were being broadcast over the radio waves. Gary's questions and my answers seemed like leg-slapping giggle fodder to most of the class at the time, most especially to classmates from farm families who knew way more about rais-ing pigs than we did. Still, Mr. Severson's teaching techniques imbedded some real knowledge in the most stubborn of students, and likely helped many become more active in group functions. Because of his coaching in the classroom, shells of shyness were cracked if not shattered, hatching new social extroverts. He was the best!!! I've written a poem to remind me of this great teacher. I wish he were here to grade it...I think.

◆   ◆   ◆

PARTS OF SPEECH
(A poem dedicated to Marlowe "Red" Severson)

When prose or poetry wants action,
Vibrant verbs provide the traction.

If an object needs a name,
Some fine noun enters the game.

Perhaps a noun is much too formal?
Find a pronoun you could warble.

All conjunctions are connective,
And are used by folks reflective.

Once your writing modifies it,
Then an adjective describes it.

Adverbs now and then are timely,
And their sounds sing out sublimely.

Prepositions are phrase intros,
Whose word tasks are added infos.

When one calls for your attention,
It's interjection intervention!

Parts of speech are well worth knowing,
If your writings you'll be showing.

◆   ◆   ◆

Unfortunately, at least for the long-term benefit to BV, he was as excellent at coaching sports as at coaching English. Tales of his talents spread across the state with the speed of a silver bullet leaving the muzzle of the Lone Ranger's six-shooter. All too soon he was offered, and accepted the position of head basketball coach at St. Cloud State College, not far from the future site of Lake Wobegon. BV's elders had good reason to be proud of this native son's accomplishments. But on the flip side of that shining heads-up coin, the town and school system suffered a major loss of both teaching and coaching talent when Marlowe Severson and his thatch of red hair atop a freckled face moved away.

In the winter of 1955/1956, BV almost experienced the loss of my sister Thalia and me. Our plight was related to milk, a substance (both straight from a teat and made from powder) that seemed to flow through much of my life during the 1950s. In order to keep enough affordable milk on the dining room table to feed the eight of us, the family bought the raw product at a bargain price from Uncle Clare, who kept a herd of milk cows as well as pigs, sheep, horses, and chickens. Milk runs meant frequent trips up the hill to his farm to fetch a few more gallons of the white life-giving lactose liquid.

We ran out of milk during breakfast on the day of a howling blizzard. School had been cancelled. As BV's dealer for Sinclair petroleum products, Dad and his snow-chained tank truck were about town delivering kerosene to homes whose owners wanted enough heating fuel to last at least beyond the present storm.

Thalia and I thought it would be fun to play the role of milkman by pulling one of our snow sleds up the hill. "Mom, can Thalia and I walk up to Uncle

Clare's place to get milk?" I asked. "I could tie a box to my sled for carrying the milk bottles."

Mother probably was delighted to get a couple of her kids out of the house. Six squirmy and energetic children cooped up together almost always led to some screaming, fighting, and tears on stay-at-home days. So, "Sure," she replied. "You two get bundled up to stay warm." She helped us put on multiple layers of clothing, warm knit hats, wool mittens, and insulated snow boots. By the time we were ready to leave, we looked more like giant mobile spindles of wool than real live people. The only exposed skin was that of two faces aglow with pairs of pink cheeks.

Thalia and I set out along the streets of BV, snow falling steadily and swirling in gusty bursts of north wind. This was January snow, not the wimpy, barely frozen stuff of October. Finding our way was easy enough, as long as neighborhood houses lined both sides of the streets. Staying on track beyond the edge of town, though, was another story. Shortly after starting up the gradual slope of River Warren's valley, we became disoriented and were barely able to move forward through the thickening snow of a ragingly relentless Minnesota storm. A few struggled steps later, blowing drifting snow reduced visibility to zero and filled our footprints and sled tracks about as fast as we were able to move. There was no clear path to follow, should we decide to retreat! I clutched the pull-rope for the sled in one hand and grasped one of Thalia's hands (clumsily, given the bulky mittens) with my other.

For what seemed like an eternity, but was probably no more than a couple of minutes, I experienced deep, spine-tingling fear for the second time in my life. The first had been just days earlier, when soot caught fire in the thin-walled pipe that exhausted the products of burned kerosene from our Unger stove to the outdoors. Watching that tube glow red-hot had frozen me with fear; I'd been unable to talk or move. Fortunately, the soot had burned away without igniting the rest of the house. Now I seemed about to be frozen in another way. "Thalia," I yelled over the high-pitched whistling of the wind, as we stumbled onward through snow as deep as our legs were long. Even healthy young kids quickly run out of energy under these conditions. "I think we're goners."

She looked at me but didn't answer. It was hard to read meaning from a facial expression that was mostly masked by a thick woolen scarf, but she must have been as frightened as I was. Our eyes watered from a continuous battering by wind and from primal fear. Ever the realist, I silently continued to paint a gloomy mental picture of our predicament. It was way too windy to carry on a decent conversation, but I was loudly thinking "Have you ever seen what happens to netted carp that spill out on the winter ice of Lake Traverse? They don't flop around for long. Maybe we'll be discovered as bodies frozen as stiff as one of those fish."

Whether motivated by fear of death by freezing or by thirst for milk, we continued to flounder along, figuring that we would encounter one of Uncle Clare's buildings if we kept going in a direction that seemed mostly uphill. Of course, in waist-deep snow, every step seemed uphill, and visibility was so limited that we didn't know whether we were actually climbing the wall of River Warren's valley or not. Tired yet tenacious, we persevered, and as the wind subsided we finally completed our mission, exhausted but safe.

I learned a lesson that day about being simultaneously patient and non-panicky persistent. The family may have learned that going without milk for a day or two is less life threatening than fetching it during a snowstorm.

That particular batch of cow juice wasn't finished causing trouble. A few days later, our sister Nina came down with a mild case of undulant fever…not life threatening, but bothersome. Following some initial confusion about how Nina had contracted this unusual disease, Uncle Clare called the town veterinarian to test his dairy herd. And so Doc Mitchell discovered that the cows were carrying the brucella bacteria and sharing this bad bug with drinkers of their non-pasteurized milk.

Why the tainted milk poisoned none of the rest of our family remains a mystery. But the mystery behind the process of pasteurization was quickly solved when Mother and Dad dusted off the P volume of the family's set of Compton's Encyclopedia. Under the heading of pasteurization they studied and took how-to notes from a detailed description of the process (attributed to the nineteenth-century French scientist Louis Pasteur) that would make our milk safe to drink. From then on, Mother's pressure cooker became a milk-pasteurizing machine following each trip to Uncle Clare's milk barn. About once a week the kitchen became a chemistry lab where temperature and time were closely monitored to be in accordance with Pasteur's instructions. The family acted out Rosie the Riveter's motto, "We can do it!"

Before a patina of dust could redeposit on the P volume, Compton's Encyclopedia provided the solution to yet another mysterious family event, this time related to me rather than Nina. This unexpected happening began to unfold on a clear-sky winter evening that seemed quite ordinary until Dad arrived home from work. The rest of us were gathered in the kitchen, watching Mother prepare a supper of fresh homemade biscuits, mashed potatoes, gravy, and pot roast. Baked cinnamon-sprinkled apples, fetched from storage in a cool-and-dark corner of the basement, would serve as a warm-and-spicy dessert. When Dad walked into the house, Mother got the usual greeting-kiss-on-the-cheek, and the rest of us heard a hearty hello.

Then: "Wendy," he said, "you have some mail today. It's from a place called Exeter. That sounds foreign to me…maybe from England." He handed me a postcard. It was one of those mass-produced tan-colored U.S. Postal Service cards, embossed with the image of a moss-green two-cent stamp covered with the smiling face of Benjamin Franklin. "Who do you know over there? Does Mr. Severson have you students writing to pen pals abroad?"

"No, dad, we don't have foreign pen pals" I replied. "I don't know who'd be sending me a card, from anywhere. I never get any mail." Dad was a continent off with his geography, as he should have realized from the lack of a foreign stamp and the postmark. That mark identified Exeter as a town in New Hampshire. The message on the card described a school there called Phillips Exeter Academy. The rest of the family gathered around as I read, first silently and then aloud, the brief note.

"Dear Wendell Duffield:" it began in a properly formal manner. At least I wasn't Wendy to whoever was writing! "The prestigious preparatory school of Phillips Exeter Academy would like to know if you are interested in attending the academy as a scholarship boy. Please respond as soon as convenient to Mr. H. Hamilton Bissell, Director of Scholarship Boys, at the address shown below." Bissell himself had signed, right above his printed mailing address.

Puzzled to an extreme, we simply sat for dinner. Before Mother could start putting food on the table, Dad spoke for us all as he pondered aloud, "What's this all about? What's goin' on here?" Family silence emphasized that none of us had any clue about what was goin' on. "Nina, would you please fetch the P volume of the encyclopedia again? First pasteurization and now Phillips Exeter. That letter's getting quite a workout, isn't it."

Book in hand, he paged toward the phill…section as the rest of us silently wondered what he would find and how long it would take. Food was cooling, and gravy cold enough to coagulate was not a family favorite. Before that could happen, he stopped flipping pages. We could see in his expression that sure enough, the academy was encyclopedia famous…so famous that it had its own entry, which Dad summarized as Mother began to set food on the table.

"It says here that Phillips Exeter Academy has a distinguished history that dates back to 1781. Gosh all fishhooks!" None of Dad's ✱ ✶ # ✳ ⚒ ! ✱ words were used at the table. "That's almost a hundred years older than BV!! It also says that the academy is world famous for preparing young boys to enter the college of their choice." A silent pause indicated a bit of mental meandering underway. "Nita, isn't that what all high schools do…prepare students for college…assuming a student even wants to go to college." Formal education beyond high school wasn't in Dad's family history, and didn't seem to be high on his agenda of what's needed to get along in life. "Sounds like an over-specialized school to me."

Now knowing the where and what of the academy, the entire family was so surprised, and more to the point confused by the postcard news that we went right to eating and forgot about Bissell and his epistle. Between bites, chews, and swallows, table conversation covered the usual evening topic of what had happened in school that day, and the unusual news that Dad was "dickering" on trading in his old 1940 Dodge tank truck for a slick 1947 International cab-over rig. Once dessert saucers had been licked clean and dishes had been washed, dried, and stacked behind the doors of wall-mounted cupboards, Dad put his plans for a truck upgrade in the background long enough to suggest "Let's think about this Exeter thing for a day or two before we send an answer to Mr. Bissell."

And so that was that…the beginning of an out-of-the-blue life-changing event left to simmer, or even get thick-gravy cold on a barely warm back burner. Though I didn't yet feel any hurt, this was the unanticipated bruising kick to my comfortably familiar life growing up in small-town Minnesota. This was my day of unimaginable surprise.

The next day, in order to get my mind around a topic I understood, I cornered Gary right before English class and told him about my idea to make more profit the coming summer with no additional work for the two of us. "Here's the thing. We know we can handle raisin' up to four pigs."

He nodded agreement and cautioned in his laconic Minnesota manner "Yabut I'm not sure I'd wanna try to gather enough food for more than that, though."

It was my turn to nod in agreement, about the difficulties of finding adequate food for pigs. "But…but what if we add sheep to the mix?"

Gary's head started to get animated again, this time in a rapid-fire motion that seemed to indicate he could see the direction my sheep idea was taking.

"We've already got a bunch of the neighborhood kids lined up to help with the milk-feeding part of our pig raising. Ya know, they'd probably fight over who gets to bottle feed a cute and cuddly lamb." We'd both seen how an orphan lamb runs to its human surrogate mother and literally attacks the nipple of a milk-filled bottle, tail wagging in exuberant delight. Talk about making a person feel important! "And here's the thing that might make this work out for us," I continued.

"Once off a diet of milk, all a growing lamb needs is grass, a little water, and maybe a block of salt to lick."

It was obvious what I was about to say next and we were both grinning like Alice-in-Wonderland Cheshire cats in the tree, drugged by the excitement of knowing a way to expand our animal-raising project.

"If there's one thing there's plenty of around here in the summer it's grass…and it's free. Maybe we could even rent sheep out as living lawn mowers. Reverend Lehner might be our first customer."

We retreated to a quiet corner to seal the plan with the farmer's handshake, and entered the classroom just seconds before Mr. Severson arrived. "Get your paper and pencils ready to write an essay on this topic," he said as he turned to face the blackboard and wrote, *What are the virtues of concentration?* My mind was so preoccupied with the possibility of raising lambs and so puzzled by what the Exeter thing might mean that I couldn't concentrate on the topic of concentration. The next day, for the first time in that class my essay came back with a large red D minus virtually shouting at me from the lead page. Mr. Severson's cryptic written comment was "What was bothering you yesterday, young man?" At the end of class, when other students were gone, I told him about the postcard from Exeter. He was so pleased that he expunged the D minus from my record.

Meanwhile, Dad had done enough sleuthing to learn that Phillips Exeter Academy had learned about me from the Minneapolis Star and Tribune. In a classic case of secret snooping, that newspaper kept a dossier of academic records for carrier salesmen and forwarded copies of those for "promising" students to Exeter and several other schools across the country. With that mystery solved, the family decided to send Mr. Bissell an answer in the affirmative.

In almost return-mail response, Bissell sent a battery of tests that the BV school principal Mr. Bambenek administered to me. He sat me down in the school library to take those exams. He said I could wave a signal to him if I needed something and locked the door. Where did he think I might go and why? The need for a pee break is all I could imagine might arise, and I hadn't had anything to drink recently.

A wall of window glass was all that separated me from the so-called study hall, where students were having a ton of fun, while maybe even studying a bit. With an unobstructed view in both directions, there was no hiding what was happening on either side of the glass. This was how and when classmates discovered the story of my Exeter postcards. This was their introduction to learning what the postcards might mean to my future…actually to *our* future. Though way beyond my imagination at the time, this was the beginning of the loss of many friendships simply because I would soon become an absentee hometown boy. This was also the moment that an invisible thin wedge inserted itself between my parents and me. That divisive tool would grow to an uncomfortable thickness as the Exeter experience influenced my life, before vanishing back into the cultural ether from whence it came.

Had I known these truths, I might have refused to take the exams, then and there. I might have signaled Mr. Bambenek to release me from my library jail so I could enjoy uninterrupted that day's study hall and the years beyond with my family and hometown friends.

Instead, I accepted the Exeter challenge and poured sweat over material far more difficult than anything I'd experienced at BV. But first, free of teacher's eyes, I unwrapped a Dubble Bubble and popped the gum into my mouth. The card was an Ernie Banks, a new one for me. Wow! He was the coolest short stop I knew. Maybe today was my lucky day.

I chose to try the math test first. Bubble gum optimism was quickly burst. How was I supposed to factor quadratic and higher-order polynomial equations when I hadn't yet been introduced to them in my BV math class?

Next came English. How was I supposed to translate into every-day words such gibberish as "When the succulence of repast reached his olfactory organ, the canine agitated his caudal appendage vigorously," when the vocabulary of my reading came from such books as "Big Red" and "Son of Big Red"…simply written stories about dogs?

Sure, I was getting an A grade in Mr. Severson's English class, but beyond recognizing the word *canine*, I hadn't the foggiest idea what was going on with *succulence, olfactory organ, repast,* and *caudal appendage.* Succulence seemed way beyond my imagination. Or might it have to do with bottle-feeding a lamb?

Olfactory? Maybe there was a misprint and olfactory was supposed to be old factory. Organ? That sounded like something to do with church to me, a place where I spent two hours each Sunday. So, maybe I was dealing with an old factory organ…one so old that the pipes needed repair. Our Methodist Church organ certainly needed work, as any even semi-sensitive ear could tell from the out-of-tune sounds it produced. Huuumm.

Caudal appendage? What in my wildest imagination might that be? I was stumped. Another case of succulence block.

Re at the beginning of a word usually meant to do over again whatever it was, didn't it? But how do you, or why would you want to repeat the past. Double hhuuuuuummmm.

I do remember thinking, as I puzzled over the sentence, that maybe some canine (always a dog in my everyday vocabulary) had somehow got his mouth around something like one of my mother's scrumptious homemade biscuits. Why the food thoughts? Maybe I was getting hungry. I *was* into the third hour of the test ordeal. Besides, dogs and food naturally go together. I was worldly enough to know that a dog will eat almost anything, anytime.

I'm sure whoever graded that test got a chuckle out of my stab at translation. Well, test instructions said better to try at an answer than to leave a blank…so dog-filched biscuit it was.

By the end of a stressful four hours, I was sure that I'd flunked the tests in spite of concentrating hard enough to produce a painful headache. Principal Bambenek mailed my efforts back to Bissell. Only days later, by way of another postcard, Mr. H. Hamilton Bissell reported that I had done well enough for him to arrange an interview with me in Minnesota.

Immersed in the youthful exuberance of an animal-raising project headed for a Harley and steeped in small-town naivety about the potential value of a Phillips Exeter Academy education, I viewed the entire Exeter/Bissell business as unwanted distracting background noise. I was far more interested in the arrival of spring birthings on Uncle Clare's farm than in some distant exclusive school whose Latin motto "Huc Venite Pueri Ut Viri Sitis" boasted that Exeter boys became men as they prepared for attending the college of their choice. Raisin' pigs and plannin' for my Harley were man enough for me!

"I hope those postcards stop comin'," I told Gary during one of our planning sessions. The mental image of being cooped up with a bunch of ultra-bookish teens (all strangers!) in an unfamiliar far-away place could not compete with the thought of soon sitting astride my own motorcycle! There were girls to think about, too. I could now afford to take a date to the movies. As the P volume of Compton's Encyclopedia made crystal clear, Exeter was and always had been an academy for boys only. Uuuugh!!

Winter days gave way to hints of spring. The last carp-filled net of commercial ice fishing was hauled in a few weeks before an ancient International Harvester chest freezer sunk to a watery grave at the bottom of Lake Traverse. The death of that appliance occurred only a few days before the onset of animal birthing on Uncle Clare's farm. Gary and I were anxious to go into production once again.

8

Harley's On Hold

When I asked Uncle Clare, "could we have any runty orphan lambs your ewes might produce this year, as well as the runty piglets?" his answer was an instant "you betcha." He understood that Gary and I were on the way to fulfilling some of our dreams. And as I guess most adults know, the less spare time that teenagers have, the less they are prone to get into various forms of mischief. Our project was creating a win-win-win situation. Adults, kids, and the commercial meat market all benefited.

Our plan for the summer of 1956 played out smoothly. We once again had four piglets to raise, and for the first time we also had two lambs in our care. Food gathering and feeding of the pigs were routine for us by now…clean the floor of Mr. Hansen's feedmill, gather village orts, and glean machine-missed ears of corn. To avoid offending the nostrils of townies, we reused the out-of-town, out-of-smelling-range pen when piglets outgrew their palace in the Kenmore Refrigerator box.

Raising the lambs was a classic Tom Sawyer experience if ever there was one in BV. Mr. Severson had assigned books by Mark Twain for reading during the past winter, so Gary and I knew how Tom had convinced his friends that whitewashing a fence was so much fun that those friends competed for the opportunity to do so. To paraphrase Twain: Work is an activity you don't want to do. Fun is what you want to do, maybe even to the point of competing to be first in line.

By the time kids in our neighborhood watched and listened to us as we demonstrated how much fun it is to feed milk to a lamb from a nippled bottle, all Gary and I had to do was explain how to prepare the milk from powder and play referee while creating a schedule of who would feed the lambs at what hours and on what days. Tom and his creator Mark would have been proud of Gary and me.

Pam Mutchler, an otherwise rather shy six-year-old who lived nearby, was almost always at the top of the daily list of feeders. She hung out with the lambs a lot. The Dusing brothers offered up their Duke Snider baseball cards to get into the lamb-feeding queue. Gary and I still hadn't scored Musial cards, and neither had the Dusings.

Pam Mutchler look-alike at lamb feeding time.

For warmth and shelter against the early spring chill, we modified an old two-hole privy that had sat unused for several years along the west wall of Dad's garage. We covered the privy's derriere holes with a scrap of plywood so the lambs couldn't fall to a filthy fate, and surrounded the building with enough fencing to create an outside playpen where the lambs could frolic during warm daylight hours.

On the subject of privies, let me share a thought that some pre-indoor-plumbing readers may also have experienced. Bluntly put, for as long as I've known about outhouses and the toilet chores carried out therein, I have never been able to understand why anyone would want a two-hole privy. I mean, who wants to sit next to a stranger (or a friend) while carrying out the sometimes noisy and very personal business transacted in a privy? The idea and the mental image of being in a situation where I might have to ask, "Excuse me, but would you please pass the role of Charmin tissue?" are way below desirable on my scale of life's activities in this world. I might be convinced that the two-holer was designed to help a parent show-and-tell a child about the lessons of potty training, *if* one of the holes was cut to the size of a small bottom. But a child of potty training age would fall into the pit beneath every two-hole privy I've ever seen, and a second hole of any size invites extra noxious fumes to permeate what's already an uncomfortably small enclosed space.

Whatever end-use philosophy underlies this two-holed relic of the pre-plumbing years, our lambs were such playful animals that they passed much of their inside time by jumping onto and from the platform created by covering the holes. When they had grown to the age of eating solid food, we released them into a nearby fenced grassy lot, which in earlier years was either a community eyesore or an unwanted grass-mowing chore. Gary and I watched the sheep thrive, without one bit of additional work attached to our schedule.

The animal-raising project was advancing smoothly that summer of 1956, until Mr. H. Hamilton Bissell again interrupted my life. His update arrived on another two-cent postcard and was therefore necessarily brief. The interview had come and gone, successfully it seemed even though my enthusiasm level registered nearly empty as he probed my personality in various Ivy League ways to determine if Wendell Duffield was of the right stuff for the hallowed halls of Phillips Exeter Academy. I read the day's cryptic message as the rest of the family sat around the supper table, this time poised to eat our favorite family meal…home-made french fries, home-made bread, small steaks from one of Uncle Clare's grain-fed beef cattle, and a dessert of home-made ice cream.

"Dear Wendell Duffield:" the message began. "Phillips Exeter Academy offers you a full scholarship for the academic year 1956/1957. Based on the results of your exams, you are qualified to enter the school at the Lower Middle level. Please advise me of your decision by August 15th." As usual, Bissell's signature appeared above his printed mailing address.

By now we had learned enough about the academy to know that Lower Middle translated to sophomore (the grade I would enter if I stayed at BV) in plebian Upper Midwest English. My increasingly confused parents, uncertain about the wisdom of sending a son off to a school and a geography completely foreign to any of their experience, chose to think quietly about the Exeter message for a few days, rather than discuss it while the fries and steaks were getting cold. We had two weeks before Bissell needed our decision. We kids certainly agreed with the decision to defer discussion. *My* fondest desire was still to become a Harley man.

We all dug deeply into supper with no further mention of the weighty, unusual offer that had arrived on a featherweight, mass-produced postcard. Each of us quickly decorated our plate with a puddle of Heinz ketchup into which we dipped finger-held french fries, one by one on their way to open mouths, marking us as commonplace rural Upper Midwesterners as clearly as Garrison Keillor's "Ketchup Advisory Board" might formally announce later on Prairie Home Companion. Could a person from such an environment fit in at elitist Phillips Exeter Academy? Would David Rockefeller, soon to be my classmate, puddle ketchup on his plate of fries?

As August fifteenth approached, the tide of confusion and uncertainty rose to saturation levels at home. Eventually, more research about the academy convinced Mother and Dad that I should try attending Exeter, at least for one year. But a family financial stumbling block the size of Paul Bunyan's blue ox Babe remained: even with a full scholarship, Dad and Mother would have to find enough "extra" money to buy me formal clothes required by the academy and to pay for travel between Minnesota and New Hampshire.

"I don't know what to do, Nita," my frustrated dad would say to mother. "Gee whillikers!" His voice sounded stressed, as though he might break into a string of pipe-thawing words. "It's a great opportunity for our son, but how can we afford the extra expenses? Even just one trip to New Hampshire and back would stretch our pocketbook thin. And it really wouldn't be fair to the girls to spend all that money on Wendy. There would be precious little fun money for his sisters."

"Well now, don't forget, Ward," our ever-calm mother reminded him more than once as the agony of facing decision-day grew. She valued education highly as a way to get along, if not ahead. "I managed to get a teaching certificate and you got some electrician training at times when our families were a lot closer to broke than you and I are today. A little money borrowed now might mean a more comfortable life down the road."

Money, money, money. That's what the big family decision hinged on. Money, the thing that had got me going on the pig-raising project in the first place, so I wouldn't have to depend on Mother and Dad for the occasional quarter. Money, the medium of exchange that separates the pine-float peasants from the malted-milk gentry. Money, the ethereal substance on paper that bankers like Mr. Zabel leverage to amass enough small increments of interest to support their cushy lifestyles. Money, an absolute necessity if I were to make the Harley dream come true.

To make a long story short, a story that I hope to tell someday under a separate cover, the brief and excruciating moment of decision in our household boiled down to how my recently created savings account could best be spent. After all these years, I can't remember the give and take of discussion around the supper table that led to a final consensus. But in the end, education beat out Harley on the priority scale. That fall of 1956, I boarded a train in Minneapolis and arrived at Exeter about a day later. Gary finished raising our pigs and sheep, got them to market, and delivered my share of gross profit to my dad, to be added to the family Exeter account.

The decision to attend Exeter led to an enormous upheaval in my life. This was definitely a harsh kick to my comfortable hometown existence. I'd never been more a couple hours' drive from home (annual Boy Scout camp in the north woods!) except in the company of the family. Now I was to travel halfway across the continent to a place called New England, but a place that would seem as foreign as old England to this hayseed farm boy.

Still, once the decision was made, my mind started to buy into the idea of unimaginable adventure. None of my BV friends had ever been on a train, to say nothing of riding one to the shores of the Atlantic Ocean. As departure day approached, I remembered a saying I'd read, or overheard in Millie's Cafe, or picked up over the radio…a trite bit of armchair philosophy. "Never try to leap a chasm with more than a single bound." So, I hurdled over to the Exeter way of life and somehow landed there upright, if perhaps on trembling legs.

What a strange and bizarre new world to absorb. Overnight, schoolmates changed from the likes of Gary Gardner and Duane Labs, to David Rockefeller and Peter Benchley. There would be no more daily sharing the odor of pig poop with Gary or witnessing the doink play of Duane. Hometown visiting speakers who emphasized well worn farming themes were replaced by the famous and learned likes of Robert Frost reading poetry about taking roads less traveled. Starched white shirts, slacks, sports coats, and neckties replaced faded and ragged jeans topped with tee shirts, or sweat shirts depending on the season. The appearance of a backwoods country kid morphed into that of a spiffily uniformed preppie. Social, economic, academic, and cultural changes that came with Exeter were immediate and stunning, yet mostly manageable.

By the end of the first Exeter year, all of my animal-raising money had been spent on the extras I needed to fit into my new and very different school world. I doubt that Mr. Zabel's Union State Bank noticed the loss, though. There were plenty of ragged edges rubbing me (and maybe Exeter?) the wrong way, but the fit proved to be smooth enough to stay through three years and graduate. As a bonus, Wendell became Duff in this strange New England world where no one knew Wendy. *Duff*...almost as cool as Red!

As another pleasant yet quite unexpected benefit, by the end of that first Exeter year the Academy's decision makers concluded that I was indeed of the right stuff to the point that H. Hamilton Bissell used money from his scholarship slush fund to buy me clothes that were more appropriate to the school's image than the sort of poorly fitting, depressingly dark formal wear available in a town like BV. In BV, putting on a suit usually indicated the need to attend another funeral; interesting styles, cuts, and colors were not appropriate for such somber occasions. We were all expected to emulate the drab sartorial look of Mr. Beaulieu. The other Mr. B bought me a tailored brown tweed sport coat with stylish leather elbow patches.

H. H. Bissell also began buying me round-trip plane tickets between Boston and Minneapolis so I could visit my Minnesota hometown for vacation breaks. I supposed the round-trip part was to buy insurance that I would return to Exeter.

I was absolutely spoiled by the financial extravagance that the Academy bestowed upon me by the time I moved on to Carleton College, to say nothing about the challenges I faced in financing graduate school at Stanford. As a Carleton freshman, my nose was roughly rubbed against the real world of paying for one's education. Eight years later, when I completed my Stanford PhD, I was frighteningly deep in debt to the U.S. Government and its program of student loans. But Mother had been correct in her advice about borrowing today for a more secure and rewarding tomorrow.

You do the math! This time the calculation is more complicated than simple addition, subtraction, division, or multiplication. But I have confidence that thinking readers will arrive at the correct answer.

PhD in hand, I landed a stable and fascinating job as a research geologist studying volcanoes at home and abroad. A few years into that career, once a dependably steady salary flowed in and education loans were paid off...you may have guessed it...I bought a motorcycle (a brand new one!) as I had so longed to do as a fifteen-year-old in BV. With newfound patience that developed as I grew older, I took time to comparison shop before buying. Somewhat ironically in light of my youthful motorcycle fantasies, I decided that I liked the quiet purr and vibration-free ride of a Yamaha Maxim more than the barking and shaking that one pays big bucks to experience on a Harley. The young boy had matured enough to evaluate multiple possibilities before choosing.

9

Food For Thought

It occurs to me that this book should convey a lesson more profound than how to shop for a motorcycle. At the risk of sounding politician preachy, if there's an underlying lesson (a politician probably would use the adjective *overarching*, to sound lofty, but I prefer the image of a firm underlying foundation to that of a teetering arch) that can be gleaned from my tale, perhaps it's to try to make your life's decisions with long-term consequences in mind, rather than giving in to the too-easy enticement of immediate gratification. It's usually worth the extra will-power and deferred pleasure. We'll all make mistakes along the way, but "thinkin' big and broadly" carries more promise of eventual lasting success.

Speaking of big: Do you remember the phrase that many French folks believe is the American national motto?…bigger is better (*plus grand est mieux*). Well, that phrase is obviously way oversimplified, if not simply ambiguous. In many situations, although not always, bigger *is* better! Thinking people understand when it's not.

About The Author

Entering Wendell, Minnesota, in 1950

Wendell Arthur Duffield was born in Sisseton, South Dakota, because his neighboring hometown of Browns Valley, Minnesota, had neither doctor nor hospital in 1941 and his mother was not interested in home birthing. Following his three years at Phillips Exeter Academy, he went on for a BA degree (1963) from Carleton College at Northfield, Minnesota, and MS (1965) and PhD (1967) degrees in geology from Stanford University at Stanford, California. Much later, after studying volcanoes for thirty-two years as a research geologist with the U.S. Geological Survey, Duffield (in "retirement") has taken up writing tales for a general readership. He and his wife Anne spend summers in the beautiful lake country of northwestern Wisconsin and winters in Flagstaff, Arizona, where Duffield is an Adjunct Professor of Geology at Northern Arizona University. The author's namesake village (see photos above and below) is a small farming community that lies between Browns Valley and Garrison Keillor's imaginary town of Lake Wobegon. The village of Wendell and the author have grown in physical stature with age. However, this village has never been called Wendy, a nickname still heard in Browns Valley when the author visits his hometown.

Entering Wendell, Minnesota, in 2004

978-0-595-37569-1
0-595-37569-3

Printed in the United States
38834LVS00007B/355